The Little Book of Little Pigs

"A realistic guide to the care and keeping of mini-pigs, with a straight forward approach."

By: Taylor Short, LVT

This book is dedicated to all of my four-legged buddies who have spent hours cozied up with me by the wood stove as I write. They are the most loyal friends that anyone could ever ask for.

My mini-pigs Maybelline & Arnold inspired me to write this book to educate people on providing a happy, healthy life for all pigs large and small.

Table of Contents

Terminology

Swine	Referring to the porcine species
Hog	Large swine of either sex (typically over 120 lb.)
Mini-Pig	TBD ...
Gilt	Female before reaching maturity; before having first litter
Sow	Intact female who has reached the age of maturity
Shoat	Intact male before reaching puberty
Barrow	Male who is castrated before reaching maturity
Boar	Intact male who has reached the age of maturity
Stag	Male who is castrated after puberty
Farrowing	Parturition (Babies!)
Piglet	What a pig is called from birth to weaning age
TPR	Temperature, Pulse, Respirations
Zoonotic	Disease that can be transferred from animals to humans
Green	Inexperienced animal (or human)
Hog Snare	A long pole applied to the snout used as a restraint device
Lordosis	Posture during mating in which the back arches downward

Foreword

As I write this book, I currently have one little piggy in my lap and one snuggled at my feet on her blanket, although I will introduce you to them later! There is no telling how many more there will be by the time I am done writing.

I have decided to write this book after seeing how many pet pigs are re-homed and taken to shelters every year mainly due to uneducated owners. My goal is to inform and educate current and potential owners on successful pig ownership so that they can get the enjoyment out of owning a pig as I do. People continuously ask me my thoughts on getting a pig for a pet, although I am also frequently contacted to take in pigs that are not working out well in their current home, so I want to enlighten people on the reality of pet pigs. Pigs can be fabulous companions BUT they can also turn your home upside down if they are unhappy. Happy pig = happy life.

This book is written from my own personal experiences in pig ownership, as well as my formal education and professional experience as an LVT, providing veterinary care to pigs around the world. Keep in mind that every pig and every situation are different. I am not above "bacon" jokes and you may even stumble across a few in the book. I am not going to use this book to express my personal morals and views on whether or not to eat bacon, ham, this, that and the other... it is merely a light-hearted publication on the journey of happy pig ownership. If one less pig gets re-homed, slaughtered, abandoned or given to a shelter than I am happy.

Chapter 1

Introduction

Let's just say that it would take up too much room to introduce you to the whole farm right now so I will just stick to the most relevant two; Maybelline & Arnold.

Maybelline is a five year old female potbelly and stands about 14 inches tall. I was contacted while I was at work that this pig needs somewhere to go before the end of the day or the owner is being evicted from her apartment. Oh joy! The [perks?] of working in the veterinary field! After a brief conversation on the phone with the previous owner, I agreed take her in sight unseen. Well, within the hour the pig showed up at my work and got to hang out with me until I went home that night. Yep, a pig and 50 lb bag of sweet feed! As shocking as this seems it is almost par for the course of my life. You just *never* know what I am going to get myself into on a daily, or hourly basis.

I have had Maybelline since she was seven months old and she has quite the diva personality. Of course it is no fault of mine that she is like that. Nope, not at all. The blueberry flax smoothies for breakfast, salads at dinner, posh leopard beds, and I wasn't going to admit it, but she even has a whole wardrobe, including a bikini. Somehow I have turned into one of *those* people.

So what the heck happened? Clearly apartment life just wasn't a good fit for her. You may ask how an adorable little pig can be so much of a burden at seven months that you are forced to give them up, even after paying a pretty penny for them. The answer is quite simple: Pigs and apartments don't mix. There may be a few pigs living the high life in an apartment but for the most part it is a bad idea, a very bad idea if you like your walls and carpet to stay intact.

Even after being around animals nearly all my life, it still amazes me how they form such strong bonds and friendships with each other. With that being said, I have to admit that Maybelline does have a boyfriend; my 1200 lb. stallion. I would not recommend allowing your 14 inch tall pig to have a relationship with a horse, although she has been persistent in sneaking out to see him whenever she can. I am not sure exactly how this ever-so-bizarre relationship started, although I know that if I can't find Maybelline I should go check in his stall.

He is one of the most gentle stallions I have ever met, so it doesn't surprise me how soft he is with her, but the true love they have for each other is a bit bewildering.

Maybelline and her boyfriend "GP"

Maybelline also has another close friend who happens to be my miniature dachshund, Ginger. Ginger's story is a book in itself, but quite simply it is by the grace of God that she is here with us today, and *walking* at that. She had a back injury and was paralyzed from the waist down before she was surrendered to me. One of my greatest concerns was having a pig living in the house while trying to rehab Ginger. Pigs typically aren't very graceful; hence one of the most common causes of death in piglets is being laid on and smothered by the sow. As Ginger began healing I started allowing her and Maybelline to interact together in the house. I couldn't believe my eyes as I observed Maybelline's response to her. She was unbelievably gentle and cautious with Ginger; motherly and nurturing. She would slowly lift one leg at a time up over Ginger and almost tip-toe around her.

They began to form a very special bond and are still best of friends to this day. Without speaking a word it was if Maybelline had a complete understanding of the situation. It is really something special to witness these relationships.

*A*rnold is another potbelly pig who I recently obtained. Only weighing in at a few pounds and standing 6 inches tall, he was already proving to be quite difficult for the previous owner to live with. His diet alone would have soon made him very ill and he smelled terrible. His ears and body were covered in yeast. Oh and potty training was a disaster which was apparent to me when I walked into their house. In no way shape or form did I need another pig but it was hard to turn down the little fuzball who was in serious need of some TLC. Needless to say he is settling in quite well. I will say though, it wasn't that Arnold was just thrown outside in the sticks and neglected - heck, he was given daily baths and cheese with grapes for a snack! Is that really what a pig needs though?

Even with the less than desirable condition he was in, I must say that he is by far the most affectionate pig I have ever met. He is just precious and loves to be held. I can't help but laugh just at the sight of him running around the house; he is just a sophisticated little man who is in constant search of attention and a cuddle buddy. I'm sure he is still having cheese and grape cravings although we had to put a stop to that before he went into renal failure and collapsed from salt toxicity.

[Side Note: My intentions are not to sound as if I am criticizing the previous owners of my pigs; they were very nice people and did the right thing by finding them

Ginger giving Arnold a warm welcome when he arrived home.

a more appropriate home, but please, please do your research before getting a pig for a pet. My examples are meant to educate on simply the basics that can go wrong even when you think you are doing everything right.]

Arnold and Maybelline didn't exactly form an immediate bond. Maybelline exhibited very territorial behavior, which I will discus more in depth later. He actually seemed to have more of a connection with Ginger. She just steals everybody's heart from the get go. Maybelline and Arnold worked through their differences, mainly jealousy issues and now they are good friends. He will sometimes lick her snout if she has leftover smoothie on it or tug on her tail for fun but she quickly puts him in his place. For the most part though I think they enjoy each others company.

Chapter 2

Little Pigs

Teacup, Pint-Size, Mini, and *even* Micro-Mini... what exactly are they? I have seen various different specifications for the titles that these little pigs are given and what it boils down to is that at the end of the day they are a pig. There are significant differences between your average hog and a Potbellied big. *Typically* potbellies will stay smaller than a hog. There are even smaller breeds within the potbellied community, which are where the trendy names are stemming from.

As far as the classifications, I typically refer to Maybelline and Arnold as "mini-pigs" since they do resemble a very small potbellied pig. Under some of the size specifications that I have seen they could most likely be further classified down into the trendy names. I don't like to get too caught up in labels for a pig staying under a certain size or weight because I don't feel that is natural or healthy. Scientifically I know that smaller breeds of pigs do exist. I also know that effective breeding can and have made different breeds of pigs smaller over time.

With that being said, unfortunately I have also observed the practices of unnaturally keeping pigs under a certain weight and intentionally inhibiting healthy growth. This I am not a fan of for many reasons. Underfeeding a pig can lead to serious health problems, including internal issues which may not be prevalent until later in life.

As far as the small size of my own personal pigs, I honestly don't know their history. I may never know if they were gradually bred down over time or if they were kept small by other means. All that I can do is give them the healthiest life possible from this time forward and hope for the best. I don't like to support a trendy industry of super teeny tiny pigs if it is causing harm or suffering to them.

This is similar to some of the trendy dog breeds that are overbred and underfed to keep them "super-duper teacup Chi-wennie-labs." I am not saying they aren't good dogs, as I have many rescued mutts myself. I even managed to acquire a Blue Heeler/Dachshund mix who got the feistiness and pizazz of both breeds! All that I am saying is that I don't think it's right to support an industry by paying high-dollar price tags for animals who are not raised humanely. There are many reputable breeders out there but unfortunately there are many that you have to weed through to find a legitimate breeder.

This is another area of research that you will need to do if you decide that a pet pig is right for you. Obviously I would recommend visiting as many reputable shelters as possible to try and adopt one from there first.

Sizing Expectations

As far as what to expect size wise, the rule I tell people to go off of is be prepared to house a pig that is around 100 pounds. Some dog breeds weigh well over 100 pounds so it isn't completely unheard of to have an animal of that size living with you. At this point there is really no definitive way of knowing exactly how large your pig will grow. When you do your homework, know the lineage of the pigs, see the parents after they are both full grown, you can generally get a good idea of the approximate size your pig will be. Even though that can give you a good idea of size, I would still strongly recommend planning for larger when determining housing size and living area. Don't let this scare you off though, as there are many mini potbelly pigs who stay in the 20-40 pound range when kept properly.

[Tip: Keep in mind though that even a piglet from a 300 pound sow can appear to be a mini-pig for quite sometime if you don't know the exact age, so don't be fooled!]

Chapter 3

Housing

If you are still in the hot pursuit of making a pig part of your family then housing is something you are going to have to consider. Both of my pigs are Indoor pigs. They do go outside with me to feed the horses and such but seem to prefer being inside. During the warmer months when I spend the majority of the day outside riding, I will leave the doors to the house open. Most of the time the pigs will have their fun rooting around outside for a bit then make their way back to their bed inside the house. Occasionally they will enjoy basking in the sunlight on the front porch or by the arena while I ride as well. I like to observe their happy place and try to cater to that. A while back I had a pig who seemed to just love the outdoors so much and would go sleep in a barn stall when she had the chance so that is what I gave her - a barn stall. I tend to be this way with all of my animals; if they want to be inside, I let them stay in, and vice versa. One of my cats stays indoors 90% of the time

"Pigs in a blanket roasting by the fire"
Maybelline and Candi (Blue Heeler/Daschund Mix)

but scratches at the door morning and night to go out and do her business outdoors. I guess the sand riding arena is a better litterbox than the one I had inside for her.

You can also play it by the season and allow them to stay indoors during the colder weather then have a covered barn, fenced yard or patio area for them in the warmer months. The wood stove is definitely a gathering area for all of my critters during the Winter.

Where ever you do make your pig's housing it needs to be piggy-proofed! I am a neat freak so I prefer to have tile floors that I can sweep and mop frequently. I have made absolute sure to keep everything up and off the floor that would seem entertaining to a pig. Even things that I didn't think would be entertaining- I learned the hard way that it was a pig's dream to get into as soon as I left for work. I had a table runner across my kitchen table that I thought was in a safe-zone. Boy was I wrong! Those tassels on the end provided Maybelline with some serious entertainment, pulling the whole thing onto the floor which included all of the stuff sitting on my table and a glass vase that shattered. Thankfully she did not get hurt or decide to eat any of the things that she pulled off the table.

I also learned that pigs are very good at opening zipped backpacks very quickly and discretely. Not 5 minutes after I got home one day and placed my bag on the floor, Maybelline brought me a half eaten chocolate protein bar that was at the bottom of my bag. Are you kidding me!? Not sure if you have ever had to give a pig activated charcoal for potential Chocolate toxicity but it is not a pleasant experience for either party. Again, thankfully she was fine.

These scenarios could have ended much worse and now I try to see even more so through the eyes of a pig, or a very curious toddler.

Both of these events happened over the course of a year, so while it sounds like she is a rambunctious terror, it was really an error on my end of not piggy-proofing better. I continue to live [with pigs] in a nice, well-kept home even with nice furniture. It *is* possible to house pigs indoors in a similar fashion to dogs, without being run out of your home if you take the proper precautionary measures.

Pigs are less destructive and onry the more exercise and activity they are provided with. Taking the time to play with your pig and find the toys that stimulate them is key to keeping them pleasant to live with.

[*Tip: Keeping a few pig-friendly toys around can help distract them from using your furniture as toys. I have found that anything that rolls, such as a ball is pretty entertaining for them. One of the toy balls with a treat inside will keep them busy for hours as well.*]

Outdoor Housing

There are various options for outdoor pig housing if that is the route you choose to go. As durable as pigs seem, they can be very sensitive to the elements and become hypothermic or hyperthermic very quickly. It is important to have a dry, well-ventilated space for their housing. Don't think that the destructive behavior will cease once outdoors... it can become even worse if outdoors also leads to less activity and attention. I think that all pigs should have frequent access to the outdoors for both physical and mental wellbeing. I know how much happier and fit I am when I spend time outdoors.

[Tip: Be sure to keep all indoor and outdoor toxic plants out of your pig's reach]

Bedding

Pine shavings tend to be a good option for bedding as long as your pig does not become too curious with it and try to eat it.

Grassy areas can be okay as long there isn't an excessive amount of lush grass, causing a sugar-overload crisis for your pig. Some will eat grass like it is candy and others won't touch it.

Concrete is great for keeping clean, although it can cause sores on their body if there is not adequate bedding over it for sleeping and lounge time. Concrete can also become very cold in the Winter, so make sure the area is well-insulated.

Dirt is probably one of the most common surfaces we see outdoor pigs housed on. It can provide a cool environment in the warm climate although it can also be the breeding ground for unwanted parasites and bacteria.

Barns

A barn can be a good place for your pig to call home as long as it is constructed properly. You want to build something durable, but also able to maintain comfortable temperatures year-round. Barns can be a more efficient option if you have multiple pigs as well.

I find that a barn with closeable turnouts is a great option because you have the benefit of sufficient ventilation, option for your pig to go in or out as they wish, and of course the ability to close up the barn during the Winter months to avoid cold drafts.

Windows that can be left open for adequate ventilation

Secure outside area for your pig to spend as much time outside as they wish during nice weather.

Outdoor housing option, with shelter for 1-2 pigs.

Make sure to use fencing that a pig can't get their snout stuck in.

Typical pig housing seen in the Philippines - nothing fancy but safe, clean and gets the job done. Make sure pigs have the option to go outside during the day.

Pasture Rotation

If you are going to house your pig in a pasture it is important to follow proper pasture care in order to maintain an ideal living space for your pig. People typically use pastures as housing when they have multiple pigs. One of the most important aspects of proper pasture care is **pasture rotation.**

Pasture rotation gives the grass and soil a chance to rest and replenish. It also gives the ground time to dry out if it is wet which is essential for parasite control. Particularly if there are multiple pigs sharing the same pasture, overgrazing the grass and over rooting the soil will deplete the nutrients. Even in a very small pasture you can, and should allow for proper pasture rotation. As shown in the diagram below, pastures are split into multiple sections. If you only have 1-3 pigs then 2 sections

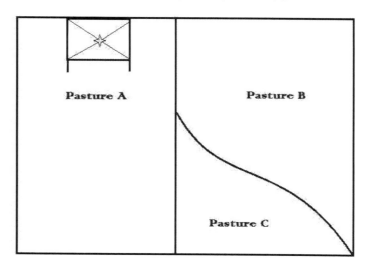

should be adequate unless you wish to do more. Take turns rotating your pig(s) through the pastures every 1-2 weeks. Make sure to keep the grass mowed down if it has grown significantly during the rest period.

Indoor Housing

Maybelline and Arnold are predominately indoor pigs although they do enjoy going outside to play. They have a litterbox which they share and and a few different beds around the house to lounge on. Maybelline prefers the big leather chairs or couch to take a snooze but Arnold is content on a bed. Many times they will snuggle together on one of the beds... it just depends on what kind of mood Maybelline is in that day. So don't be surprised of your pig jumps up on your couch for some snuggle time with or without you.

[Warning: This can cause human guests to go into a panic attack...for some reason it isn't something they are expecting when they are sitting on someone's couch and up jumps a pig! Go figure.]

I like to keep a few different types of beds around for them. I find that they like the circular beds with sides on them, as it gives them the feeling of security. It seems to mimic the feeling of another fellow pig buddy next to them for that warmth and comfort. I also have a couple larger flat memory foam beds for when they want to lounge with one of the dogs. Pigs like to burrow when they sleep so giving them a blanket on top of their bed is greatly appreciated.

Litterbox

There are various bedding options on the market that you can use as litterbox material. I will say that with trial and error, I have found that that compressed pine pelleted bedding works by far the best. Low-dust, low to no odor and seems to last the longest between changes and cleaning. This can be found at most local feed stores and is relatively low-cost.

There are other materials that can be used such as pine shavings, shredded paper, and many other new and improved litterbox materials on the market now. I tend to stay away from anything scented or dusty, such as sandy cat litter because I have seen many pigs show sensitivity and allergies to it. Some pigs will try to eat it, or even refuse to eliminate in it if it is scented.

Pigs can be very particular about their "restroom" so don't hesitate to change up the litterbox material if you are having constant potty-training issues. I've even had a pig refuse to use the litterbox when I changed brands of compressed pine pellets. As soon as I switched back it immediately fixed the problem. I do not condone this type of "snobby" behavior, although it is important to know how they think.

Compressed Pine Pellets

There are different styles of litterboxes you can use. When your pig is small, you can simply purchase a litterbox at the pet store which is made for cats. As your pig grows, they may outgrow a cat-sized litterbox. One of the problems I found is that the walls of a cat box can be a bit too high for some little pigs to get into.

I personally don't like the look of litterboxes so I hand-crafted a litterbox to go with my home. It was actually a fun and rather simple project. Oddly enough I always get compliments on it!

Maybelline & Baxter cuddling by the wood stove on a snowy day.

Don't be surprised if your pig even stakes out a favorite chair. Maybelline was headed to tell Baxter to get off "her" chair.

I'm still not sure how he puts up with her...

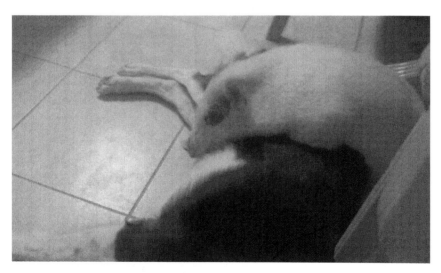

Another one of her favorite sleeping spots - on Baxter's back.

Maybelline trying to sneak a sip of Pumpkin Spice rum at our Christmas party. You really have to keep an eye on her when there is anything pumpkin around! Of course she came finely dressed in her favorite leopard sweater.

You can always count on your pig to keep you company while you cook.

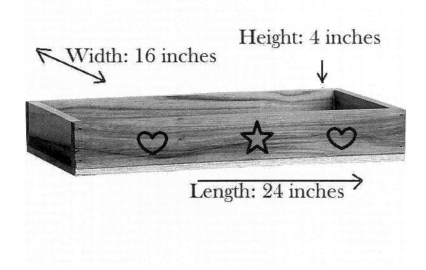

HAND-CRAFTED LITTERBOX

Supplies Needed:

Wood 4"tall X 2" thick X 36" (or amount for desired length & width)

Nails or wood glue

Plastic storage container (I found it easier to find a container first with similar dimensions then built the wooden box around it.)

Decorative materials of choice:

~ Wood can be covered in fabric, hair-on-hide, painted, etc.

For example, to match my western-theme room I adhered 2 horse shoes to my box.

Chapter 4

Nutrition

I have to say that this is probably the most important topic of the book and the aspect of pig-life that I am most passionate about. I feel that there are so many negatives that we can change simply with proper nutrition. Not only is nutrition a key element in growth and good health, but also has a strong effect on attitude and overall happiness.

I believe that you are what you eat and I feel that it directly translates to the pig world as well. If you are fed nasty piles of old slop then you are going to look and smell like a nasty pile of old slop! The concept is quite simple: Food is power. When choosing your pig's diet you have the power to help eliminate unnecessary body odor, keep them happy (nobody is in their best mood on an empty stomach or constipated) and even help prevent major medical issues.

With that being said, you can choose how far you want to go with selecting the proper diet for your pig. You can make meals at home or buy a pre-made pelleted feed at most local feed stores.

[Tip: I would strongly recommend consulting with a veterinarian who specializes in mini-pigs to help you create the best nutritional plan for your pig. There are many different factors to consider such as protein, fat, carbs, fiber content and more that will depend on age, growth, activity level and any pre-existing medical conditions.]

By nature, pigs are omnivorous which means that they can not make their own protein. If you do make a homemade diet it is crucial to ensure that adequate protein is obtained. Pigs in the wild obtain their protein from worms, bugs, deceased animals, etc. Rooting outside helps pigs obtain the necessary minerals from the ground and may occasionally give them a bug or two to munch on. It shocked me the first time I saw it but some pigs will chase a fly or bug around the house to eat it.

I personally do a mixture of homemade meals along with a high-quality pelleted feed made specifically for mini-pigs. The amount of pelleted feed depends on what I am feeding for my homemade meals and treats. I know that with a lettuce salad they are not getting all of the protein and nutrients they need just from that salad. Some of the necessary nutrients that a pig's diet should contain are protein, fat, carbohydrates, fiber, selenium, riboflavin, pantothenic acid, choline, B12, biotin, folic acid and vitamins A, D, E, K. In addition to that, additional requirements can be needed during different stages of growth. reproduction and aging.

A maintenance diet for an adult pig should contain around 12% protein, 2% fat and 15% fiber. Younger pigs will need a slightly higher protein level, usually around 14% during their growth stages. It is important to follow the directions on the feed bag for your pig's age and weight. If that amount doesn't seem to be adequate for you pig, then re-evaluate but it is a good place to start.

There are many benefits to feeding a high quality, commercialized pelleted feed. Convenience is definitely high on the list and also ensuring that you are feeding your pig complete nutrition; meaning that no additional supplements need added to their diet. Some brands of feed will also contain urinary acidifiers and Yucca extracts to help decrease urinary calculi and ammonia in the urine, which is a plus.

Potbellied pigs should **not** be given feed made for commercial hogs due to the fact that it is designed for rapid weight gain in a relatively short time period. Any Equine or Livestock Sweet feed is not appropriate either.

[*Tip: It is important to gradually make changes to a pigs diet; preferably introducing the new feed over about 7-10 days.*]

Meal Plan

For breakfast I typically will feed oatmeal and bran with a fruit smoothie. The smoothie deal started because I make a smoothie every morning for my breakfast and Maybelline caught on. She would start oinking and getting excited when she heard the blender because she knew what was in it. Then Arnold caught on. I obviously make their smoothie first without any milk or dairy products. There are other ingredients that I will occasionally add into their smoothies:

Flaxseed – Supports skin and immune system health. Ground flaxseed is ideal. Whole or ground flaxseed needs to be mixed in with food to minimize choking.

Wheat Bran – High in fiber and protein, so it helps them feel full longer. Needs to be fed as a mash to minimize choking.

Rice Bran Oil – Improves coat quality and can add shine. Rice bran oil is high in fat so limit use if you are trying to get your pig to loose weight.

[*One of Maybelline's favorite treats is popcorn. I make it from scratch in a small amount of coconut oil. It is a healthy and fun treat but make sure there is not any salt, sugar, or butter on it!*]

Maybelline's Blueberry Smoothie

1/4 Cup fresh blueberries

1/4 Banana

1/4 Cup Unsweetened Applesauce

1 Tbsp. Flaxseed

Add ingredients together in blender. Puree until fully mixed. Enjoy!

Arnold's Apple Almond Smoothie

1/8 Cup Almonds

1/4 Apple

1/4 Banana

1 Tbsp. Flaxseed

Add ingredients together in blender. Puree until fully mixed. Enjoy!

Other great snack options:

Cucumber	Sweet Potato	Squash	Broccoli	Green Beans
Tomatos	Apples	Carrots	Bananas	Strawberries

[Tip: Dog, Cat or Guinea pig food are NOT a good alternative to a mini-pig's diet.]

Pigs often enjoy parts of fruits and vegetables that are less desirable to us, such as carrot tops, strawberry tops and the ends of green beans. I like to keep a tupperware in the fridge so as I am preparing meals to cook I can just toss the remainder of the veggies in there. Most fruits and vegetables should stay fresh for a few days and you can usually get a few more days out them for your pig as long as there is no mold on them. I think this is a fabulous concept not only because it is a convenient, healthy, low-cost pig food, but it also minimizes food waste.

[Warning: Under no circumstances should your pig eat any high-sugar or fatty treats; from ice cream to fried fruitcake, cheese to bacon - if you think this is healthy than you are a bit mistaken. This type of food is not heathy to be feeding to a pig, even as an occasional treat.]

Dinner

Dinner typically consists of a salad with various vegetables and a specialized pig pellet as a topper (much healthier alternative to croutons.) No dressings, spices or sauces should be added to their food. I usually make a salad for

myself for dinner anyway so it is easy to make a few more while I'm at it.
My animals are not normal - all of my dogs beg for salads too.

It is crucial to maintain a healthy, proportioned diet for your pig. If you wish to feed your pig treats or snacks, set aside a set daily amount for them. Often those frequent little snacks can add significant caloric value to a diet very quickly.

If you have food in your hand chances are they are going to act hungry - possibly even ravenous. This does not indicate that your pig needs more food. As long as your pig is receiving proper deworming, maintaining an adequate weight, receiving the proper nutrients and caloric intake, you should not need to be concerned. Ideally, pigs should be fed proportioned meals twice per day. They should not be allowed access to an unlimited supply of food, also known as "free feeding."

Pigs are similar to humans in regards to their metabolism. Some 100 pound pigs can maintain their weight on 1/4 cup of food per day, and others need much more than that to keep a healthy weight. On the flip side, some pigs who are overweight can have their food amount cut in half without shedding a pound. It is important to frequently evaluate the individual needs of each pig long before it becomes a problem.

Maybelline & Ginger patiently waiting for breakfast.

Enjoying a fresh tomato from the garden.

Common Foods To Avoid

Spices - Sweets - Fish - Onions - Dough - Grapes

Rhubarb - Chocolate - Avocado - Salty Foods - Dairy

Grazing

Grazing is recommended for all pigs as as long as the grass is not overly lush with increased protein and sugar content, such as Alfalfa. For a pig who has never had grazing access, or has not grazed in awhile you will need to increase grazing time gradually. Grass in the early Spring as well as in the Fall can be particularly high in sugar content so be mindful of the time of year and environment you are grazing them in.

Daily turnout example: Day 1: 2 min, day 2: 5 min, day 3: 7 minutes, and so forth.

Once your pig's turnout time has been gradually increased, you should be able to leave them outside for extended periods of time without having them gorge themselves on the grass. You should also cut back on their normal feed if they are out grazing for any significant amount of time. You can fulfill their grazing requirements even in a fenced back yard. When we hear grazing we typically imagine a huge pasture with rolling hills, but that doesn't need to be the case. Some pigs should not be on grass at all due to medical reasons so make sure to ask your veterinarian if it is appropriate for your pig.

Rooting

Have you ever seen a pig rubbing their snout on the ground or even on your leg? This is called *rooting* and is a natural part of a pigs life that should not be discouraged. Pigs root to get the essential nutrients they need from the ground, such as selenium and iron. Pigs also root as a form of enrichment. Pigs are definitely smart enough to distinguish where it is acceptable to root, so that boundary should be established by you immediately. If there is an area you do not want them to root, make sure to keep it consistent that it is an off-limits area. If you allow them to root in a particular area one day then not the next they will become very confused.

Some people don't mind if a pig roots their hand or leg - I personally think it is cute as long as it is gentle and respectful. Sternly telling them "No!" will correct this behavior if it is something that you don't want them to do. What initially starts as cute, harmless rooting can also lead to nipping or biting so just make sure to stand your ground and always expect respect.

For the enrichment aspect of rooting, I like to provide my pigs with a rooting box inside which consists of a wooden box that contains balls, blocks, large stones, and other toys in it for them to root. Providing them with a rooting box can minimize the temptation to root your carpet or other off-limits areas. It is important for them to be allowed time outside for rooting as well to obtain nutrients.

[Tip: If you find that your pig is eating too fast you can hide their food/treats in the rooting box so it takes them longer to eat. Just make sure the wood isn't treated or that there is anything else in there that could be harmful if ingested.]

Drinking

It is imperative that your pig be provided with fresh drinking water at all times. Pigs like to go back and forth from drinking to eating which can make a bit of a mess. They can also be a bit messy when simply drinking their water, but a kitchen or bath mat under their water dish keeps things tidy.

To encourage drinking, a very small amount of apple juice (sugar-free, 100% juice) may be added to their water. Make sure that this is only a temporary, and if -needed practice otherwise they will become dependent on tasty water. Just think - if a child is only given juice and sweet drinks, they will surely turn their nose up when water is offered. You can also add a piece of frozen fruit to their water bowl to encourage drinking. Again, make sure they do not become dependent on this! With that being said, you shouldn't need to add anything to the water, as pigs naturally tend to drink enough water.

If pigs do not get adequate water intake, serious medical issues can arise. If your pig suddenly stops drinking water it could be a sign of something more serious. If water consumption does not resume with encouragement then I would strongly recommend a visit to your vet. This point also holds true for food consumption; if your pig refuses to eat there is definitely something wrong.

[Tip: Refrain from giving your pig any energy or sports drinks
as it can cause an electrolyte imbalance.]

Chapter 5

Training & Behavior

"A cat looks down upon a man, a dog looks up to a man, but a pig will look a man in the eye and see his equal."
WINSTON CHURCHILL

Training and behavior have a significant impact on how pleasant your pig will be to live with. The majority of questions I am asked regarding issues people are having with their pigs directly correlate to improper or complete lack of training. This isn't always someones *fault* per se, sometimes older pigs that people adopt just never received that foundation when they were younger. The issues that often arise from owners having difficulty training younger pigs is simply misunderstanding them and not knowing how their mind processes information.

Another issue is lack of training when they are younger because they are just so darn cute that you can't punish them. Yes, this happens far more frequently than you would imagine. I personally have seen little untrained, disrespectful pigs grow up and, well, those are the ones who are abandoned, rehomed (hopefully), or otherwise no longer part of the family. That is what I want to help minimize.

I think the greatest factor in training pigs and enjoying them is truly *understanding* them. Often times mini-pigs are directly compared to dogs. There are many similarities in behavior and even training techniques, although the mind of a pig tends to process information differently. Honesty, if you want to compare them to help relate to them - compare them to humans. I have found that they are far more similar to humans, from processing information to health and nutrition, than any other animal I have met. It can take a little while to understand them but once you are on the same page with them it will be a fun, loyal and trusting relationship.

The quote written by Winston Churchill stating that pigs see you as equal could not be more true. The meaning of that quote wasn't necessarily meant to appear in a training section of a little pig book, although it was well-said. Contrary to dogs whom look up to you, a pig sees you as one of the 'herd." I find that pigs will push your buttons more than a dog and are quicker to have disrespect for you if that line isn't initially drawn. Pigs can be very affectionate and respectful with proper training and care.

Swine Psychology

Pigs are highly intelligent animals; fourth smartest animal in the world last I heard. They really are impressively unique creatures. They are inquisitive, curious, social, compassionate and loving animals. Pigs are also surprisingly very sensitive emotionally therefore they don't want you to be upset with them. This is important to keep in mind when disciplining them. They do have feelings! These are often qualities that we don't get to appreciate with pigs since the general consensus is that pigs are just a bunch of nasty hogs plopped down in the mud out on a farm.

It isn't just potbelly pigs who exhibit these emotions and intelligence. I once had a Hampshire pig (large breed) who was equally as smart, trainable and loving. She even had a whole wardrobe as well. It simply depends on how they are raised.

Similar to humans, pigs are very capable of evaluating other people and animals. They are intuitive; possibly even more so and more accurately than humans. They can sense if you dislike them and they do remember negative events rather well. This can be helpful when correcting unwanted behavior although you don't want them to start viewing you as the aggressive herd member who is constantly being mean to them. They will then just shut you out. Effective discipline is essential, although building trust and love is equally important.

Pigs tend to think "herd" minded, with a strong understanding of which herd members are more dominant or lower in the pecking order. Like I mentioned earlier - in their eyes you are now part of the herd, or they are now part of your herd. In essence, we have similar social groups but instead of herds we refer to them as friends and family. Since most pigs are caring, social, affectionate and nurturing by nature, generally they want to be friends with you. Once you are "in" their circle of friends than you are good. It's getting "in" that you have to first see eye-to-eye and prove loyalty and trust to accomplish.

Part of the whole *understanding* them concept means that there has to be communication, as with any successful relationship. In order to effectively communicate with your pig you have to first understand that all of the grunts, squeals, and snorts are actually a complex communicative language. It may seem annoying or frustrating at times if you are unsure what they mean but these are not just random noises. They are great at communicating a variety of feelings, emotions, wants, needs, and other important messages.

My two favorite grunts are the high-pitched, soft oink that they have when they run up to you and are happy to see you when you walk in the door after being at work. I just can't help but smile regardless of how stressful my day was. The other grunt is almost comparable to the pur of a cat... when they are cuddled up next to you and softly say "ahhh" that they are perfectly content and comfortable.

Just like learning any new language, it does take some time to catch on but once you do it's fun. The best thing about learning this language is that you don't have to oink or grunt back for them to understand you. Yes, they understand clear english or whichever language you are training them in. Studies have even shown pigs to understand words in a conversation and I have observed this as well. I'm not sure if they understand the whole conversation, depending on the complexity, but I know that they do pick up on certain words. I once was having a conversation with someone and said that I was going to go outside. Not realizing that Maybelline was listening, her ears perked up and she went to the door ready to go outside with me! Moments like that are very intriguing and it makes me wonder how much more they really know and understand than we give them credit for.

So with that being said, keep in mind as you embark on your training journey that they are often far smarter than we give them credit for. They do not appreciate having commands shouted at them and being *told* to do something. Give them a chance and actually teach them. It all goes back the the Golden Rule:

~ Treat them the way that you wish to be treated. ~

Operant Conditioning

Operant conditioning is a type of learning which is based on the fact that the consequences of a behavior will increase or lessen its frequency. It encourages associating desirable or undesirable consequences with certain behaviors. Behavior, both negative and positive, that is rewarded will increase in frequency. This also serves true that unpleasant behavior will lessen or halt in frequency based on the undesirable consequences. Basically: *reinforcement increases behavior, punishment decreases a particular behavior.*

This tends to be the most realistic and straight-forward approach which pigs and I understand the best without blurred lines. "Do right - reap the benefits." Oh and do wrong... you're going to wish you went with the first option.

What are acceptable forms of reinforcement and punishment?

I feel that reprimand should be catered to each situation and each individual pig. For example, if you are administering punishment to a pig who just bit you and you are unprepared, an immediate vocal and clapping punishment would be able to have the quickest and most effective response. Now if you have been having trouble with your pig biting and are prepared, then a better punishment might be a small squirt of water to the face while stating "BAD!" The reasoning behind this is that if you were to run and get a squirt of water after your pig bites you then come back and squirt them in the face they are going to be completely confused and think you are crazy. Remember they think of you as one of the herd - you are now the crazy lunatic cousin of the herd with a water gun.

Regardless, the quicker the punishment can be implemented, the better chance you will have of your pig learning that what they did was unacceptable. If your pig urinates on your floor and you don't find it until hours later the punishment will typically not have much effect. The same holds true for reinforcement - the sooner it's applied after the incident the better chance it has of sticking with them.

	Reinforcement/Praise	Punishment
Verbal/Auditory	Sweet tone "Good girl!"	Firm tone "NO! BAD!
	"Good Potty!"	Loud clap of hands
Physical	Soft pet or scratch	Firm tap to the shoulder
	Food treat	Small squirt of water

You will need to determine what works best for your pig. Which ever methods you chose to use **consistency** must be maintained in order for any training regimen to have positive, long-lasting results. I also like to make a point of using a verbal training aid first, such as "No!" so that eventually you will only have to use a verbal aid because they will assume there is worse to come if they don't listen. The same goes for positive reinforcement. You should associate positive physical praise with verbal praise as well so that eventually "good girl" will let them know that they have done a good job and not necessarily need a treat to accompany it.

If you have repeatedly punished your pig (more than 5 times) for the same problem then a different route needs to be taken. First evaluate your consequences and approach; is your punishment firm enough? Is your reinforcement poor? Are you even offering them praise or is everything "NO! BAD! NO! BAD!" and they think they can do no right?

In some cases acting out can be the sign of a medical problem that they are trying to tell us. It is important to "listen" to your pig and notice abnormal signs that they are trying to tell us something. For example, urinary issues can initially present as inappropriate urination outside of the litterbox. Repeatedly or all of a sudden becoming destructive could be a sign of boredom or anxiety for one reason or another. If you are ever the slightest bit concerned that there could be something medically wrong then play it safe and take them to the vet for a quick check up.

Expectations

The minimal expectations for your pig should include:

- Eliminating in appropriate area

- Tolerate (and hopefully enjoy) daily handling

- Friendly towards people and other animals

- Adapt to change without too much difficulty

- Can be left alone for a reasonable amount of time without misbehaving

- Not being destructive, territorial or aggressive

- Ability to travel comfortably in a kennel or trailer

Age

One of the factors that plays a relevant role in training is *age*. There are pros and cons to both getting and older pig or a younger pig. As far as training a pig, it is much easier the younger they are. One of the benefits to getting an older pig though is that they should already be trained and you can just focus on the fun and companionship side of ownership. BUT, getting an older untrained pig will be quite challenging. It definitely can be done but the saying "pig-headed" didn't just appear from thin air. Older pigs can be very set in their ways and reluctant to change. In some respects you can cater to their preferences, although some get to be so "pig-headed" that they act out and become defensive when they are asked to do something or don't like something that you do.

As far as litterbox training goes, if an older pig is not already litterbox trained it can be very difficult and frustrating to get them to understand why after all of these years you want them to eliminate in a box, in a house, when they have been used to going outside in the dirt or shavings all of their years. I have seen some older pigs take to a litterbox rather quickly, but that is typically not the case. Younger pigs seem to take to litterbox training much better.

Pigs of all ages tend to be rather smart so they seem to catch on to things fairly quick. This can be a benefit when teaching them new tricks but can also have a negative effect when they learn that there is FOOD in the fridge! Overall I wouldn't recommend a younger pig over an older pig or vice versa. To me they a fun at all ages. You just need to decide if you are up for the training stages that younger pigs will go through.

Biting

When pigs act out it can be shown through various behaviors, although biting is the most common. I've never really seen a pig "nip" either; a bite is a bite. If you think about it though, naturally biting is their main defense mechanism. Cows can kick, cats can scratch, horses can kick, bite, rear and then some, but anatomically speaking, biting is all pigs really have going for them. Pigs don't usually give much warning before biting either. They may grunt or squeal first but it is not as consistent as it is in other animals giving noticeable warning. For example, snaring, lunging or growling in a dog can be a strong indication that they could bite soon. In a horse pinning of the ears is a strong indication that a kick or further negative behavior is coming if the stimuli continues. Pigs can show standoffish or tense body language before biting but it is usually subtle and takes time to learn to recognize.

Knowing that biting will most likely be their form of a negative response, you can be prepared. By prepared, I mean that you can be ready to correct it if it should ever happen. Under no circumstances (unless they are being hurt or attacked) should a pig be allowed to bite. It may look cute when they are young with their adorable little bottom lip and squishy little snout but it can be extremely dangerous as they get older. Pig teeth are not something to mess around with.

As with many vices, biting can usually be stopped if it is promptly corrected when it happens. One of the most common reasons for a pig to start biting is due to hand feeding them. When you give them food or treats by hand you are teaching them to associate your hand with food. This often goes unnoticed when trying to figure out why they are biting. WE often create these problems and never even realize it. The most simple and straight forward fix: NEVER feed them by hand.

To be sure that you are not going to accidentally implement this behavior you can put all food or treats into their food bowl to feed them. With that being said, this book is meant to express the reality of mini-pig life so I will be honest with you; I just can't get enough of that squishy little snout. I do occasionally give my pigs treats by hand. I have spent a lot of time building respectful relationships and teaching them proper behavior so thankfully I don't have any issues with them biting or associating my hand with food.

To correct the negative behavior of a pig trying to bite, often a loud hand clap and firmly stating "NO!" "BAD!" will do the trick. Another appropriate punishment for biting is to squirt them with a small stream of water while saying "NO." This isn't meant to be a water boarding punishment, but simply more of a quick, unpleasant shock to deter them from engaging in that behavior again. Make sure not to get water in their nostrils, eyes or ears though. Very rarely will it escalate to the point where you need to take further action and make contact with them. If need be, a tap to the shoulder while saying "NO!" will correct it. Never use anywhere on their face or snout for "tapping" punishment as it will make them scared and head shy.

Socializing

Socialization is important for the mental well being of your pig. Some pigs can thrive as an only child but they do need to have some sort of contact or friendships with other animals and people. I currently have two extreme opposites of pigs; one comes running up to new people when they walk in the room and the other shy's away. I don't know if something specific previously caused her to shy away from new people or if that is just her personality. She is definitely getting better but still needs to really get to know someone before cuddling up with them. Such a lady.

Other pigs that I have had fall somewhere in the middle. They typically don't shy away from people, but don't expect them to come jump up on you with a wet welcoming kiss the way some dogs do. Guarded but curious will most likely be their initial response to meeting new people.

Pigs do not like situations being forced upon them. When introducing them to new people (or animals) it should be done slowly and somewhat on their terms. Let them come to you rather then going after them. Whatever you do - never chase a pig! You can pretty much guarantee ruining that relationship forever if you do. I don't necessarily recommend using food or treats every time they meet someone new either. This can lead to associating people with food, which can lead to biting and essentially, viewing people as only a food source. I personally want to be thought of as more than just a food source. Again, realistically speaking if it is going to make someone's whole day to feed a treat to a pig by hand, then just proceed with caution and common sense.

It will surely be a stronger and more respectful relationship in the end if it is built on multiple positive experiences rather than just food. Effective ways of human socializing with a pig can include a belly scratch or softly petting them, taking them on a walk, playing with them with their favorite toy or simply just letting them sniff your leg while sitting there letting them feel out their curiosity.

Pigs should definitely be encouraged to socialize with other animals as well, even if it isn't a member of the porcine species. My pigs have always formed close bonds and friendships with my dogs and even cats. Keep in mind when you are introducing them, in most cases your pig nor your other animals have ever seen or heard anything like this before! Don't be disappointed if they don't click from the start. That is the point of socializing and gradually building that relationship. Very rarely do we become best friends with someone in the first five minutes of meeting them so we shouldn't expect our animals to either. My animals are very used to me bringing home all different types of animals so not much bothers them anymore. They may not be best friends immediately but they have learned to at least tolerate them and show basic respect initially. The more socialized they are the more accepting they will be when there is a new face (or snout) in the house.

When beginning to socialize your animals it is always good to error on the side of caution and expect the worst. It is beneficial to have two people that are able to help if the introduction does not go well. Start with both animals on a leash, or your pig in a kennel and dog on a leash of your pig isn't leash trained yet. If it is a positive introduction then you can proceed with them off leash and out of a kennel. Having worked with animals of many different species and breeds, I have learned that they are very intuitive and pick up on your emotions very quickly. They can sense fear, confidence, anxiety and most importantly tranquility. Keep this in mind when you are not only around animals in general, but during a new introduction you want the animals to sense that you are calm and confident, implying that there is nothing to fear.

Even when all of the proper steps are taken to socialize your pig occasionally there will still be some resistance on their end. This may be due to a previous negative experience (and in that case we need to strive even more to build their confidence) or simply that is just their personality. If your pig is not socializing well with people and you have tried the methods suggested earlier then you can try a retreating approach. Simply take a step back and try not to push yourself on them too much. Give them a quick scratch behind the ears or on the belly then walk away. Keep it a short and sweet positive experience. Doing this multiple times throughout the day will teach your pig that you only have positive intentions and want to be friends. Like the guy who keeps asking you out and wont back off - all you want to do is distance yourself from him! So don't be that creepy overbearing dude.

If your pig is showing resistance to animal socialization then we have to take a look into the mind of how the other animal is viewing the situation too. There are many great, well-written 1000+ page text books explaining more in-depth psychology of animals. For simplicity and to keep you reading I am not going to touch on all of the elements of psychology here. The subject is very interesting though and I would advise you to educate yourself on the matter if you are truly interested in understanding an animal's perception.

Fear is the most common factor on a pig's end due to the fact that they are prey animals and really don't have a strong defense mechanism. Some dogs are actually bred to herd pigs and livestock. Some dogs instinctively just want to eat bacon! Some are just so mesmerized and intrigued by the squeals and mannerisms the pig makes that they want to play with it all day as if it is a squeaky toy. So we can't really blame the pig for being fearful of these animals that would be considered predators to them in the wild can we?

Out of all my dogs I personally have a dog that resembles at least one of all of the examples I gave. They have all learned to play nice and not treat the pigs as if we are trying to survive in the wild. Even Ginger, my dachshund had to learn that the pigs are not her 24/7 squeaky toy to chase around the house. Contrary to her belief the squeakier will eventually run out of "squeak" just as the stuffed toys do.

[Note: Pigs are very sensitive to stress which can actually lead to an acute death, therefore they should never be chased or tormented by another animal or human.]

Horses are prey animals as well, but they seem to fear the pig more than the pig fearing the horse. The unknown smells, movement, and sounds that a pig makes is typically what will spook a horse. We don't need to focus too much about directly socializing horses and pigs, as I wouldn't recommend housing them in the same stall together due to the size difference. If your pig is going to be housed in a barn around horses though I would do some distant socializing so that your horse doesn't see or hear the pig for the first time while being ridden.

Most of the time cats and pigs will just leave each other alone and you don't need to push the relationship. I have never seen a pig or cat show aggression towards each other. One of my cats licks the pigs and likes to cuddle with them which is a bit odd but as long as it doesn't cause any harm to either party I will just let it be.

Socialization should be fun for your pig. From my observations it is typically the other party, either human or animal, who needs to work on how they are approaching the situation. Humans who subconsciously radiate fear or dislike of pigs most likely have no idea how smart our little oinkers are and that they can clearly pick up on that. Other animals who are radiating dislike for a new pig in their "territory" can also be sensed by your pig. Encouraging multiple positive experiences and interactions over time is your best bet for success in this scenario.

Desensitizing

After you have created a strong foundation of respect and socialization, desensitizing should come fairly easy for your pig. The younger your pig is the easier desensitizing will be, although all pigs should be desensitized. Desensitization refers to getting your pig accustomed to important situations and procedures that could one day even save their life. It is crucial that your pig be comfortable traveling, being touched, handled and preferably tolerate mild restraint. The reason is that when your pig needs veterinary treatment the last thing that you or the veterinary staff should have to worry about is trying to handle your untrained pig squealing and flailing around uncontrollably. In severe situations, once at the vet sedation can be used if needed. Although keep in mind that it should not be relied on because some medical concerns could be exasperated with sedation, therefore making it an inviable option.

There is a simple fix for this - desensitizing. When you are playing with your pig, occasionally apply mild restraint; putting pressure around them (big hug!) picking up a foot then setting it down, touching them all over - ears, face, belly, flank area, and being held (if possible due to size.) Make these sessions short and sweet - just another part of the day. The goal is for these tasks to not phase your pig or throw them into a squealing panic attack.

Leash/Harness Training

On the subject of desensitizing, getting your pig accustomed to being walked on a leash with a harness is very beneficial. This is not only a great benefit when taking your pig in for veterinary appointments, but it also provides a way to exercise. Taking your pig on a walk is beneficial in many respects. Getting your pig out of their normal environment and going for a walk can be a fun adventure for them that improves mental and physical well being. It can be a fun adventure for you too as long as they are properly leash-trained. If they are not leash trained then it will only be a fun adventure for your neighbors to watch as you parade by their house with a pig throwing a major temper tantrum.

This aspect of training is very similar to leash/harness training a puppy if you have ever experienced that. First you will need to find a well-fitting harness for your pig. There are specialty harnesses made for pigs that are shaped specifically for their bodacious bodies. When they are younger you can use a small dog harness for them. Once you have selected your harness place it on them and allow them to walk around freely to get a feel for it. Make sure that it is not constricting, but also not loose enough that a hoof could get caught up in it. I promise you they will not like that.

Some pigs will not be as receptive to the idea of a foreign object on them all of a sudden, especially around their neck. A foreign object around their neck in the wild would be a very fearful situation. Knowing that is how they could perceive this, it is your job to make it a pleasant experience, offering praise and helping to eliminate any potential fear.

After they are comfortable wearing the harness you can hook the leash to it. For training I prefer to use a 6-8' leash to keep close contact although a retractable leash can be used later on for walks if preferred. When starting to leash train your pig apply slight pressure in one direction of the harness. When they make a move (even the slightest move) in that direction release the pressure. In doing so you are rewarding them with moving in the direction that you just asked of them. You should also be turning to the left with your body to show them what you want. Ultimately they should be able to mimic your movement while walking... you turn left, they turn left with you... You stop, they stop.

In addition to encouraging movement with light pressure on the leash you

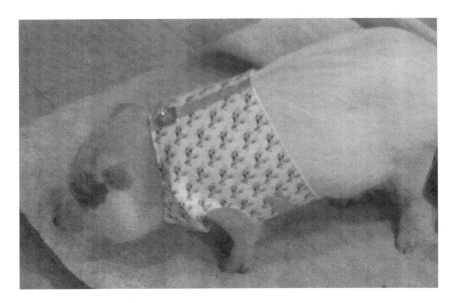

Maybelline sporting a vest that also doubles as a harness to easily attach a leash to.

can use voice commands in combination. Say "walk" to walk, "whoa" or whatever word you choose for stop, and so forth. You will have a walking companion in no time! If you are getting resistance with your pig moving forward, I find that they respond better when you ask them to go left or right first, rather than forward. After some lateral movement you can then transition into asking them to walking straight ahead. If you have access to trails pigs tend to enjoy walking on them with a change of scenery and fun exercise. The footing is also easier on their hooves than concrete.

[Tip: It is important to always use a harness for a pig rather than a neck collar to avoid constricting their airway.]

Housebreaking (Litterbox Training)

This part should come fairly easy if you have already been teaching your pig right from wrong. Like I previously mentioned, pigs want to be clean animals so most of them actually enjoy having a litterbox. If you have ever potty-trained a puppy you shouldn't have any problem litterbox training a pig. One of my pigs who had never seen a litterbox before walked right over and used it as soon as I put it down. Don't expect it to be *that* easy though.

The first step is to select an appropriate sized litterbox for your pig. Next you can select the material that you want to use for litter. Place a thin layer in the box; too little will not absorb the urine and too much will get on their legs and make them feel dirty when they use the box. It is best to place the litterbox in an area where it is somewhat quiet and low-traffic so they can have their privacy. Try to keep the litterbox in the same area and only move it for cleaning.

As soon as it is constructed place your pig in the litterbox and say "go potty." They may jump right out or root around in it for a few minutes but either way is fine. Don't rush them or force them to stay in it, as we want this to be a positive experience. While they are in it I will also say the word "litterbox" or say "good litterbox" so they can learn to associate that word with that area. It sounds silly but it has been fail proof on my end time and time again. If they happen to use the litterbox the first time you put them in it immediately offer verbal praise and even a treat would be ideal.

Plan B: If they do not eliminate in the box the first time you put them in it don't be discouraged. If you know your pig well enough catch them when they look like they have to go to the bathroom then put them in the litterbox at that time following the same steps as mentioned above. Right after eating is also a good time to try again. The goal here is to praise them when they use the litterbox as much as you can. If your pig happens to have an accident during this time say "No! bad! Get in your litterbox!" At this time place them in their litterbox and give them praise. Even if they go to squat down or start to eliminate outside the litterbox it is not to late to redirect them.

If you are still getting resistance try switching up the litterbox material or even move it to a different location. Consistency is the key to successful litterbox training and if you keep with it you will have a well trained little pig in no time!

Chapter 6

Veterinary Care

This portion of the book is to give you a brief overview of preventative health care as well as other common medical conditions that commonly arise in potbelly pigs. The content is not intended to replace or override the medical advice recommended by your veterinarian.

Many people prefer to administer preventative care themselves and there is nothing wrong with that choice. I have experienced both ends of the spectrum from administering treatments at home as a naïve pet owner, to working with some of the best doctors in the country. From that standpoint I am going to give you my two cents.

There are many factors to consider when administering your own preventative care and the greatest factor is *education*. It is crucial to educate yourself on what you are doing, how you are doing it and most importantly why you are doing it. Nobody was born knowing the tricks of the trade or became a successful doctor from spontaneously practicing hear-say treatments from 40 years ago. They have put in the hard work and effort to professionally *educate* themselves. This is how the best of the best gain their knowledge so why shouldn't you?

For the average mini-pig owner looking to administer their own preventative care I am not suggesting that you go through vet school for it, but rather to educate yourself by other professional means. This does not include internet blogs and what a friend told you they did with their hogs way back when. There is nothing wrong with obtaining advice from a friend who happens to have experience with pigs, the problem comes when such information is not accurate or in the best interest of *your* particular pig. The reason that I am touching on this subject is because I continuously see misinformation being relayed to naive owners who are just *trying* to educate themselves but are getting it from the wrong source. Books are a great resource to get your baseline information but ultimately the most accurate medical advice you are going to receive is from a qualified professional examining your pig right in front of them. This is why finding and building a strong relationship with your veterinarian is so vital to the health of your pig.

Contrary to popular belief, many veterinarians will be supportive if you elect to provide a portion of the preventative care at home and will even provide you with the proper dosage. The majority of the time vets will recommend that vaccinations and such be administered by them because things can go wrong - they have seen it with their own eyes. Not until I educated myself did I realize how many things can go wrong - simply with "just" giving a vaccine. The actual act of giving it... do you know where all the veins and arteries run and how close you could be to hitting one? Then what could come next...a vaccine reaction? Anaphylactic Shock? In which case there typically isn't even enough time to make it to the vet without loosing them.

I am not trying to scare you away from administering preventative care yourself - just simply stressing the importance of properly educating yourself first. Often times your best bet for education can be right in front of you - your vet. Just talk to them, tell them your concerns and your wishes. Most importantly have respect for them. They are not trying to make a buck on your $20 vaccine, they genuinely care about practicing the best medicine possible which is what they went to school for so many years to do. If you don't feel that your current vet is the best fit for your pig then find one who is, particularly one who has experience working with pigs.

I am sincerely passionate about enhancing the veterinary community as a whole, which includes the people who support the veterinary community: pet owners. The more educated and aware you are of a potential problem with your pig the greater chances there are to fix it promptly and successfully.

Normal Vitals

It is important to know the basic parameters of normal vital signs for your pig. This will give you a baseline to reference to should they ever become ill or show abnormal behavior. When taking vital signs, pick a time when your pig is relaxed and in their normal environment, not worked up after playing outside or in the heat.

Temperature is taken rectally via a digital thermometer with a small

amount of lubricant, although if you are not comfortable doing so that is completely understandable. I would recommend recording their pulse and respirations though. Each pig will have their own "normal" although it should stay between the following ranges for young to elder potbelly pigs. Neonates and geriatric pigs will vary greatly.

Temperature: 99.0 - 102.0 degrees F

Heart Rate: 65-95 beats per minute

Respiratory Rate: 10-24 breaths per minute

To obtain a **heart rate:** place your hand over their heart on the left side of their chest, just behind their elbow. Heart rate is recorded in number of heart beats per minute (BPM.) You can count the number of beats over the course of one minute or count the number of beats over 15 seconds and multiply that number by 4 to get your rate. To obtain **respiratory rate:** the easiest way is to watch their chest rise and fall while breathing. Each inspiration and expiration sequence is counted as 1 respiration. (Breath in, then out = 1) Respiratory Rate is recorded in number of breaths per minute (BPM.) You can count the number of breaths over the course of one minute or count the number of breaths over 15 seconds and multiply that number by 4 to get your rate.

Reproductive Health

	Females	Males
Age of puberty:	4-6 Months	2-4 Months
Estrus:	2-3 Days	N/A
Gestation:	106-113 Days	N/A

Female pigs will have an estrus cycle similar to many other mammals, with the length of their cycle averaging 21 days. Estrus only occurs for 2-3 days which is less than most other mammals. When your pig is in heat you will most likely notice her vulva become swollen and observe behavioral changes. She may become moody, dominant or even overly affectionate. *Maybelline used to mount your leg and everyone thought it was so funny but realistically hooves on your leg is no laughing matter.* This is not a time to allow unwanted behavior but to just be prepared for what is to come. The behavioral changes may be the only changes you see, as vaginal bleeding during their cycle is not observed. You may notice a small amount of vaginal discharge of either a clear, pink or cloudy mucous. Foul odor or abnormal color may indicate a problem or infection. *Lordosis* may also occur during this time which is what you will notice if you gently press down on her back and she assumes the mating position with a very passive attitude. Not something I would recommend doing to your pig, although if you are petting her and she exhibits this distinct behavior you will know what it is.

Females generally reach puberty between 4-6 months of age, although it can occur sooner, especially when around a boar. I would just play it safe and not allow unaltered males and females to interact after 6-8 weeks of age for risk of pregnancy.

Spaying your pig is strongly recommended as it will eliminate multiple unwanted issues. Pigs who are not spayed tend to develop attitude problems and can become very mean and dominant during estrus. There are also many health benefits to spaying your pig such as eliminating pyometra, uterine tumors, and STD's. Although piglets are adorable, there are plenty of pigs out there that need homes already. If you want a very young pig, you can usually find a pig who was accidentally bred for one reason or another and adopt a piglet via that route.

Males on the other hand reach puberty as early as 2-4 months of age. Once they reach puberty they seem to be on a 24/7 mission to find a girlfriend. Males also have pheromone-secreting salivary glands which are used to sexually stimulate female pigs. It has a very distinctive (foul in my opinion) odor.

It is strongly recommended that you have your male pig neutered (castrated) to eliminate unwanted behavior and odor. They will me much more docile and friendly to humans as well as other pigs if they are castrated. The sooner it is performed, the less amount of time there is for any of the "boar effects" to become prominent. Typically castration can be performed as early as 6 weeks of age.

Life Span

The average life span of a potbelly pig is around 10-15 years, although there have been some reported to have lived a quality life well into the 18-20 year time frame. Unfortunately these statistics are for potbelly pigs in general and the life span of many smaller versions or "mini-pigs" have a significantly decreased life span. Some go on to live long healthy lives into their teens, although many have not lived more than 2-5 years. This is a harsh reality to take into consideration.

To date there are no definitive explanations for why mini-pigs are living such shortened lives. From my personal views on this matter - it is not normal. I don't feel that there are that many incompetent owners who get a pet pig and are that oblivious to something wrong with their pig. Sure there are a few, but it is hard to believe that this is the case for every young pig who dies. Unfortunately, mainly due to cost, sometimes ethics, necropsy procedures are not being performed on the majority of deceased pet pigs. Even in the cases where a necropsy *is* performed, there is often little to no evidence of the cause of death, although typically ruling out anything infectious, toxin-related, trauma inflicted, neoplasia, or foreign body obstructions. In many cases reported by pig owners there are minimal, if any abnormal signs preceding death.

In my opinion, and strictly opinion, it seems as there could be some significant congenital abnormalities in these pigs. Not all, but some. Could this be the result of the pigs who are gravely malnourished to stay so small through how many generations of this act? Granted it is not the case in ALL mini-pigs, but enough to prompt my curiosity. I wanted to briefly touch on it though since it is a contributing factor in mini-pig ownership and the reality is that it *can and does* happen.

As far as the pigs who are symptomatic and die at home before they can get to the vet or pass shortly after arriving at the vet, I feel that some of those cases can be prevented as well. Some - not all, but to me that is good enough to write about if we can save one more pig out there by educating owners on just how critical some symptoms are.

Some of the common symptoms and indications that your pig should be seen immediately include:

-Open-Mouth Breathing / Panting / Gasping for Air

- Bluish or pale coloring around snout or on gums

-Wheezing / Crackling noises while breathing

- Inappetence

- Lethargy

- Vomiting

-Bleeding

[One night while working an ER shift I took a call from a lady asking why her pig was not eating or drinking today? I explained to her that there could be numerous reasons but I strongly suggested that she bring him in immediately to be seen. I strongly stressed the urgency but the lady never could grasp that... no matter how many potential life-threatening concerns I listed off that it could be, she still refused to see it as an urgent matter. The next morning I called to check on him and he had died. The lady began crying and apologizing to me saying, "you were right I should have brought him in - I didn't realize how serious it was." I genuinely felt bad *for the lady who just lost her little pig, and I honestly don't think she realized how serious it was. Regardless, it doesn't change the outcome.*

The reason I share this with you is that this is one of the areas that pigs are different than dogs or other pets. Not that it is right, but the reality is that many people don't bring a dog into the ER, or even to their general practice vet for that matter if they stop eating or drinking for a day. Sure something is wrong and they need to be seen, but it rarely leads to an acute death. The difference in pigs is that it is a very serious symptom that has a high chance of leading to death quickly if left untreated. This doesn't mean that every pig who has inappetence is going to die, it simply means that it is a strong sign they are ill and need to be seen by a vet promptly.]

Normal vs. Abnormal Behavior

We discussed behavior previously, although we didn't touch on it pertaining to health as much as training. Abnormal behavior is generally one of the first signs that your pig will give you if something is medically wrong. Even the slightest change in behavior should be monitored closely. I have seen numerous pigs with various different diagnoses acting normal the day before then flat out and gasping for air the next....then right back up at it a few hours later for some. I don't know if we should call this dramatic or the other extreme of being stoical and enduring. Have they had something going on and they are so stoical about it that we don't know? Do they get a belly ache and think they are dying? Sounds outlandish but I have seen it occur time and time again. I suppose the point that I am trying to make is that you need to act quick if you notice something wrong because even the most simple of health concerns can send them into a fizzle. Pigs typically don't give you the gradual warning that other pets do when they are ill. Even when they do give you warning signs, they are relatively subtle.

Pigs do enjoy their R & R and can be known to sleep more than say, dogs but they should still be bright, alert, and responsive when they are stimulated. As mentioned with vitals, each pig will have their own "normal." Surprisingly pigs can be very active. They may sleep a little more often than other pets but watch out for the little firecracker when they wake up!

Often times this is a surprising trait that people do not realize about pigs until they have one running around their house. I frequently hear them referred to as toddlers and I have to support that. My pigs are always on the go; curious, playing with something, *trying* to get into mischief, rooting through the toy box, hiding my shoes, and the list goes on. This is the part of pig ownership that I find so comical. They are just so smart and clever and seem to be on a constant mission to prove it. Then I ask Maybelline, *"Where is my shoe?"* The response I get is silly little high-pitched oinks as if she is laughing at me. I can't help but chuckle even though I am going to be late for work if I don't find my shoe soon. This is very normal behavior for pigs, especially the younger ones so consider yourself warned.

I would go so far as to say an *inactive* pig is abnormal. If this is their "normal" it may not be an immediate medical concern to go rushing them to the ER, but it should be addressed. Possibly they are obese, depressed, bored, lonely, or all of the above? A pig who is not curious or on the go at least occasionally would be a red flag to me. If your pig is known to be very active then, either gradually, or suddenly has a decreased activity level, that is a good indication that they are not feeling well.

On the flip side, if your lazy pig suddenly becomes anxious or hyperactive it could be the sign of a toxin exposure or other medical concern.

Shying off or suddenly sleeping in a new distant location, such as in the back of a closet can also be a sign of abnormal behavior. Even pulling back or becoming less social than usual can indicate something is wrong either mentally or physically. Really get to know them - observe their "normal" personalities and behavior as frequently as possible. That will provide you with the best indication when something is abnormal and should be further evaluated.

Veterinary Care

Part 1: *Preventative Care*

Many deadly diseases and common complications can be prevented by proper preventative care. Some of the procedures and protocols, such as recommended vaccinations are going to be partially based off of geographic location and other individual contributing factors. With that being said, please discuss all preventative care decisions with your vet prior to administration.

Hoof Care

Being diligent with your pig's hoof care can lessen the occurrence of lameness issues as they get older. Generally speaking, their hooves will need to be trimmed 2-3 times per year.

Where your pig is housed and exercised will play a role in determining how often they will need to have their hooves trimmed. If they are inside on carpet or other gentle footing then you will probably need to have their hooves trimmed more frequently than a pig housed on concrete flooring. The amount of exercise they get on pavement, dirt or gravel can help keep their feet trimmed naturally too.

You can learn to trim their hooves yourself although I would recommend seeking professional help if there are any abnormalities in the hoof such as soreness, foul odor, deep cracks or splitting of the hooves. For superficial cracking, dryness is most often the cause and can be corrected with moisturizing hoof dressing or cream. This can be purchased at most local farm animal supply stores. Whether you trim your pig's hooves or have a professional trim them, your pig should be comfortable with their legs and hooves being handled.

[Tip: Coconut oil is a great natural alternative to hoof cream
... and works wonders!

Ear Care

Occasionally pigs will get debris in their ears and need their ears cleaned. It is important not to put fluids directly down in to their ear canal as you would a dog, because they can not shake their head forcefully enough to get it all out. The best way clean your pig's ears is with a wash cloth dampened with warm water or a gentle ear cleaner. Preventative ear cleaning lessens the chance of ear infections.

Dental Care

Pigs are susceptible to gingivitis, periodontitis, tooth abscesses and other forms of Periodontal disease. Nutrition plays an important role in minimizing and preventing Periodontal disease. Yet another reason we want to limit their sugar intake. With proper nutrition your pig may not need to have their teeth cleaned, although there are some pigs who do require annual teeth cleaning. This is typically an anesthetic procedure performed by your vet, although if taught at a young age you can use a tooth brush with "piggy toothpaste" to brush them yourself. Prevention is a much better route than treatment after the fact when it comes to dental health.

[Tip: Foods such as crisp apples & bananas can help keep teeth clean naturally. The fibrous consistency of a banana peel is great for helping to keep teeth clean due to the high magnesium content. They will typically stand there and chew on it for a while so that aids in cleaning the teeth as well. Feed banana peels in moderation due to the fact that the peels are not as easily digestible.]

Tooth Eruption

Incisors   (deciduous) Birth - 2 weeks
                (permanent) 8 - 18 months

Canines   (deciduous) Birth
                (permanent) 8 months -1 year

Premolars   (deciduous) 2 weeks - 8 months
                (permanent) 12-16 months

Molars   (permanent) 4 months - 2 years

[Note: Don't be surprised to find a tooth around the house or in their food bowl - this is normal during the teething process.]

Tusk Growth

Depending on the age of your pig you may notice that they have **tusks.** The tusks on female potbelly pigs are typically much smaller than they are on the males. The tusks of females rarely get long enough to even protrude out of their mouth. Males will grow tusks that are much more noticeable, which protrude from the sides of their mouth around 2 years of age.

Not all tusks will require trimming. If they are posing harm to your pig, other animals, or people then trimming is definitely a sensible option. Tusks may pose a threat if the pig is aggressively using their tusks. There are other cases in which tusk trimming is advised, such as the dental arcade being asymmetrical and causing the tusks to wear or rub abnormally.

If you do elect to have their tusks trimmed then it needs to be done with as minimal stress for your pig as possible. This typically includes sedation at your vet. If sedation is not used for trimming the tusks, and your pig moves or jerks back with the tools in his mouth it can cause permanent damage. Pigs have also been known to accidentally inhale the tusks which for obvious reasons is not a good situation. So, for everyone's safety it is strongly advised that you have your vet trim the tusks. If you are asked how much you want them trimmed, I would suggest not going any shorter than 1/2 inch off of the gum line. Going any shorter tends to cause soreness and greater risk for infection

[*Tip: If you are having your pig anesthetized for tusk trimming it is also a good time to tackle their other preventative care, such as teeth cleaning or hoof trimming while they are still sedated.*]

I have heard the words "tusk removal" thrown around quite a bit, even before someone gets a pig. Removing the tusks on a pig is no cake walk of a procedure. The tusks are deeply associated with the jaw bone, commonly causing it to fracture if the tusks are removed. I would strongly recommend that you do not have your pig's tusks removed unless it is absolutely warranted for medical reasons.

Many complications can arise after the procedure including severe infection and can be extremely painful even for weeks after. If you are looking to have the tusks removed for any reason other than a serious medical concern, then I would reevaluate your reasons for getting a pet pig. Some people think they are doing it for the safety element but forget that they have a mouth full of teeth as well that can be used to bite. You would be much better off spending the time and money training your pig proper behavior.

Vaccines

Specific vaccines are not approved for potbelly pigs, so those available for commercial swine are substituted. Vaccines can be started at 4-6 weeks of age. Most initial vaccines are followed by a booster 3-4 weeks later, then annual vaccination thereafter. Some vaccines may be boostered more frequently if your pig is in a high-risk area for the disease. It is important to monitor your pig closely for negative vaccine reactions which typically will occur within about 15 minutes after receiving the vaccine until as long as 48 hours following. Negative vaccine reactions are relatively rare, although need to be addressed promptly if it occurs. They can range in intensity from mild redness or soreness surrounding the injection site to lethargy, hives, facial swelling, fever, vomiting or any other negative reaction the body chooses to show. If your pig shows any reaction to a vaccine it is important to notify your vet. Often times there are pre-medications that can be given before their next set of vaccines to eliminate vaccine reactions.

There are certain vaccines in which your pig may be more prone to having a reaction to. If your pig has a reaction, it is typically due to one of the vaccines even if it is a combination vaccine. Leptospirosis and Rabies seem to be the most common to cause a negative reaction in potbelly pigs. Based on how intense of a reaction they have it may be beneficial to eliminate or decrease the frequency of that particular vaccine in their rotation. You will just have to weigh the pros and cons to determine what is best for your pig.

Rabies Virus Vaccine

There is an extremely low incidence of Rabies confirmed in swine in general, much less in potbelly pigs. Although, this does not mean that they can't contract the disease. Currently it is not a vaccine requirement for pigs in most states, and rarely a recommendation. Vaccine protocols are constantly changing as new information becomes available so please discus the need to vaccinate for Rabies with your veterinarian, especially if your pig is housed outdoors.

Tetanus Vaccine

Tetanus is an infectious disease which is caused by the bacteria *Clostridium tetani*. You may have also heard this disease referred to as "lockjaw." That is because the inability to open the mouth or move the jaw is one of the distinguishing symptoms. Muscle spasms followed by continuous muscle contractions are typically the first symptoms to present.

Tetanus is contracted by a contaminant introducing the bacteria into the body. This can be via unsterile surgical instruments, bite from another animal, puncture wound, or other various trauma. This disease is easily prevented by annual immunization and preventing contaminated wounds as much as possible. In most cases it is required before a surgical procedure in your pig, including alteration. This is a relatively safe, low-cost and highly effective vaccine which all pigs should receive. It is cheap insurance for the possibility of contracting the fatal disease. Keep in mind that humans are also susceptible to Tetanus.

Erysipelas Vaccine

Erysipelas is a disease most commonly characterized by severe skin discoloration, with the patches appearing diamond-shaped. Hence the reason it is commonly referred to as *diamond skin disease*. Initially the lesions may appear as just a patchy rash but usually distinguish themselves soon as diamond-shaped. Erysipelas is caused by the bacteria *Erysipelothrix rhusiopathiae*. In addition to the unsightly skin component, it can also cause septicemia, arthritis and endocarditis. It is strongly recommended that your pig be vaccinated for Erysipelas.

Parvovirus Vaccine

DO NOT use a canine Parvovirus vaccine to vaccinate your pig

Porcine Parvovirus (PPV) is a disease in pigs which is exhibited in reproductive failure. Unless your pig is going to be around other pigs or in a breeding program then it may not be crucial that they receive this vaccine. I wanted to mention it though because it is probably the most common vaccine I get asked about. Many people hear about Canine parvovirus and believe they should give the same vaccine. Parvovirus does not affect pigs the same way that it affects dogs. Reproductive abnormalities, most frequently the death of piglets before they are full term, is the most common clinical sign. This vaccine most likely will not be recommended for your potbellied pig.

Leptospirosis Vaccine

Leptospirosis is a zoonotic bacterial disease and has various different strains; *L. pomona* and *L. bratislava* being the most common in pigs. This is a very serious disease which most mammals are able to contract and spread. It is transmitted most often through the urine of wildlife and can linger in the environment long after they are gone. This means that if an opossum ever comes through your yard, the risk is there. Most commonly Leptospirosis in swine is detected when there are reproductive abnormalities, such as poor productions and late stage abortions. In regards to mini pigs, anemia and renal failure can result, with early symptoms of lethargy and bloody urine. Leptospirosis can be deadly if untreated and can be contracted by both males & females of any age. I would highly recommend that Leptospirosis be in your pig's vaccination routine.

In mini pigs this seems to be the most likely to cause a vaccine reaction, with a fever being the most common symptom. This is merely something to watch out for not necessarily a reason to avoid vaccination in an otherwise healthy pig.

Bordetella Vaccine

This disease does not exactly affect pigs the same way that it affects dogs. The two main pathogens associated with the disease are *Bordetella bronchiseptica* and *Pasteurella multocia*. They can occur independently or as a dual infection, causing atrophic rhinitis. The initial signs seen are nasal discharge and sneezing, although it can also lead to growth retardation. This infection can also lead to pneumonia if left untreated, especially in young pigs. Ideally the mother of your pig would have been vaccinated prior to farrowing since the disease is very contagious from nose-to-nose contact with other pigs. Regardless, I would recommend vaccinating your pig for this disease annually or biannually depending on the risk of exposure in your location.

Do not use a Bordetella canine vaccine to vaccinate pigs.

[There are many other swine vaccines available although these are the most common that are administered to mini pigs. If your pig is going to be around other pigs, such as on a pig farm or used in a breeding program, then you may need to vaccinate for additional diseases.]

Deworming

Pigs should be routinely dewormed starting at 6-8 weeks of age regardless if they are living indoors or outdoors. Pigs living outdoors or in an area where parasites are more prominent may need more frequent deworming. Most dewormers come in a palatable oral form that can be sprinkled over food, squirted into their mouth via syringe or injectable.

Ideally you should have a fecal sample analyzed to see if your pig is currently harboring any internal friends. This can be done fairly low-cost at your vet. I highly recommend this when getting a new pig so that you can eliminate any parasitic problems before they are able to manifest around your property. Some worms, such as Roundworms are zoonotic, with pose a higher threat to children in the household due to the frequency of touching things then accidentally putting their fingers in their mouth. Getting a fecal sample analysis is also very beneficial because you are able to confirm which worms are present, therefore selecting the appropriate dewormer.

There are various different types of dewormer on the market but many of them only treat specific types of parasites. For obvious reasons it would help to be administering the right dewormer. Ivermectin is one of the most popular dewormers in pigs due to it's broad spectrum properties. It can be used to treat both internal and external parasites with relatively low side effects. Pyrantel Pamoate and Fenbendazol are other types of dewormers that your vet may suggest you rotate with.

Make sure to pay close attention to the strength of the dewormer you are using and follow dosage instructions precisely. Many of the swine dewormers are made for very large pigs so the amount of it you may need for your mini-pig will most likely be a micro-mini dose. Even a slight overdose of dewormer can lead to serious neurologic disturbances and even death.

Skin Care

There are many different factors from nutrition, to parasitic infestation and even allergic reactions from the environment or a grooming product that can cause skin issues. Often times it is a simple fix when tended to promptly. Determining why your pig is itching can be the difficult part but I would recommend getting a professional diagnosis before treating the condition.

The reason I suggest a professional diagnosis is due to the fact that some of the skin issues that cause pigs to itch, such as mange are **zoonotic.** This means that the condition can be transferred to humans. Therefore the sooner the proper treatment is administered, the less chance you have of becoming itchy yourself.

Another reason I suggest confirming what you are treating prior to treating, is that some treatments may actually make the condition worse if you are treating for the wrong thing. There are many over-the-counter soaps, sprays and creams that claim to relieve itching, although I have seen many that cause skin to dry out worse or even cause an allergic reaction.

It is important to use products that are specifically made for or approved for pigs. Even though a pig's skin appears tough it is actually quite sensitive to topicals. Bathing your pig is something that should also be part of your grooming routine, although it is equally important not to bathe them too much. A good rule of thumb is not to bathe them more frequently than every 2 weeks. If your pig seems to stay clean longer then I wouldn't rush to give them a bath. The longer the better between washing so the natural oils don't gets stripped away. I will also apply a small amount of baby oil or coconut oil to their skin after I bathe them. Less is more when it comes to ingredients in grooming products and try to refrain from using any scented or perfume products.

Maybelline's Lavender Body Oil

- 1 Spray Bottle

- 5 Drops Lavender Oil

- 8 oz Baby Oil

- 1 tsp. Honey

Mix ingredients together and lightly mist on skin. Make sure to apply a small amount to one area first to make sure your pig is not going to have an adverse reaction to it.

~

[This might be TMI but if I spray this oil on my legs and don't spray any on Maybelline, she will rub her back on my legs to get some on her. She will actually do this with any lotion if I don't put any on her first. It's hilarious.]

"Excuse me but I need a bath too!"

~

[Tip: Another part of your grooming and skin care routine should include brushing. A soft-bristled brush works best and they tend to enjoy it quite a bit.]

Coat Blowing

The good news is that pigs do not drastically shed their coat on a daily basis which makes it nice when they are living inside. You may find a few stray hairs but it is nothing like the shedding that most dogs have. That is until they experience **coat**

blowing. Luckily it only happens 1-2 times per year depending on your pig and the climate they are in. During this time they will naturally shed out their whole coat and the hair will fall out quicker if you are brushing them. This happens over the course of about 10-14 days and at the end they will be nearly bald. If you are not expecting them to do this it can be a bit shocking and scary to see you pig loose so much hair. Not to worry though, it will all grow back in and is usually very soft and fuzzy during that time. Keep in mind that their skin will be more sensitive during this time so make sure to apply sunscreen if they are outside and moisturize any dry skin.

Arnold's After-Sun Soothing Spray

1/4 Cup Aloe Gel

1/4 Cup Witch Hazel

5 Drops Peppermint Oil

1 Spray Bottle

~

Mix ingredients together in spray bottle and lightly mist on skin. Make sure to apply a small amount to one area first to make sure your pig is not going to have an adverse reaction to it.

~

Veterinary Care

Part 2: Common Health Concerns

Dry Skin

This seems to be by far the most common problem that pigs develop. [Someone once told me that they had to give up their pig because she was using the coffee table to scratch on because she had such horribly dry skin. She ended up breaking the coffee table which made them upset (yes she had some obesity issues as well.) They tried bathing her a few times but it didn't seem to get better.] And this was the pig's fault how?

Many pigs I've seen that have terribly dry skin, have never received any kind of treatment for it because many owners think that "it's just one of those things that pigs get." Unfortunately I have heard this over and over again. Yes, it is very common in pigs to develop dry skin but definitely doesn't have to remain that way.

If it is truly just dry skin you can try to treat it first at home if you wish, although it is important to have your pig examined if it doesn't resolve soon. Dry skin can occur for many reasons. If your pig is housed outside or goes outside frequently, sun damage can occur. Especially if your pig is light-skinned you should apply sunscreen when they are outdoors. Hydration is a key element as well so yet another reason to make sure fresh water is available at all times.

Chlorhexidine-based shampoo is very broad spectrum against many of the organisms that can lead to skin irritation. Try bathing your pig with a small amount then allowing them to dry completely before applying a skin moisturizer formulated for pigs. If you are not able to locate a pig-specific moisturizer, baby oil or coconut oil works well too. You may also look into adding a fatty acid supplement to their diet, such as flaxseed, to improve dry or flaky skin. If you don't notice relief shortly after

If you are ever suspicious of a parasitic condition, play it safe and wear gloves, make sure to wash your clothes thoroughly and any skin that came into contact with the pig. Ideally, don't let them come into contact with your skin.

then I would recommend having them seen, as it could be a parasitic factor causing the dry or irritated skin.

Mange

Many pigs that have itchy, irritated skin which doesn't resolve with your average dry-skin treatment are commonly diagnosed with mange. A quick skin scraping performed at your vet can confirm if your pig has mange. Sarcoptic mange is the most common type of mange found on pigs and is transferrable to humans.

Pigs who are infected with mange become very uncomfortable with the severe amount of skin irritation that Sarcoptes causes. They will try to scratch themselves on any object in sight. For their comfort and to minimize the chance if it spreading to you, it is important to initiate treatment as soon as possible. Ivermectin is commonly used for the treatment of Sarcoptic Mange.

Lice

Pigs are very susceptible to lice and it is a common contributing factor to skin irritation and itching. It is more common on large pig farms, although mini-pigs can harbor the little parasites as well. Make sure to check your pig's skin closely if you are getting them from a location with other pigs on the premises. There are multiple effective treatments for lice on the market such as insecticidal spray, pour-on, and even straight Ivermectin. Make sure to read the label closely and apply in a well-ventilated area. Also keep in mind that after the application, the lice are going to be falling off rapidly. An area which can be thoroughly sanitized is ideal.

Fleas & Ticks

Thankfully fleas and ticks are not as common in pigs as they are for dogs and cats. Pig skin does not create an attractive environment for these external parasites, although that isn't to say that they can't get them. Ticks do not particularly like to latch on to thick pig skin but I did pull one off of Maybelline after walking her on a trail. Just do frequent tick checks if your pig goes outside, but you should not need to apply a monthly flea/tick prevention as done with other pets.

Alopecia

Alopecia is the loss of hair. Alopecia in pigs can happen for a variety of different reasons although dry skin, mange and lice are high on the list for things that will cause alopecia. If your pig has patchy areas of hair loss or complete hair loss make sure you have ruled out those conditions first. Of course make sure to rule out coat blowing too depending on the time of year.

Diarrhea

Stress, infection, parasites, diet, toxicity, and the list goes on for the causes of diarrhea. It is important to identify the factor causing it to make sure you are administering the appropriate treatment. Above all, you need to make sure that your pig is being replenished with the fluids and electrolytes that they are loosing with multiple episodes of diarrhea. Dehydration and electrolyte abnormalities are frequently the cause of death rather than the infection itself, especially in young pigs.

Escherichia coli commonly referred to as E. Coli is definitely high on the list of concern when diarrhea is observed. E. Coli is very common in younger pigs, even in piglets less than a week old. It is transmitted via fecal-oral route and is zoonotic so make sure to wash your hands thoroughly after handling any pigs with diarrhea. Coccidiosis (Isospora suis) is also a common cause of diarrhea but more commonly seen with high-volume pig farms and poor sanitation. Yellow to green liquid stools, occasionally containing specks of blood are one of the distinguishing symptoms.

Something as simple as a diet change or an addition of a new food can be enough to cause diarrhea as well. Make sure to make diet changes gradually and implement new foods in small amounts to decrease the chances of GI upset.

Adding a probiotic into their diet can help with diarrhea if all other infectious, toxin and parasitic factors have been ruled out and your pig is still having diarrhea. It can also help while recovering from any of those conditions but make sure the probiotic is not going to interfere with the prescribed medication they are on.

Constipation

Constipation is one of the other commonly reported issues that people have with their potbelly pigs. Again, also one of those conditions that people hear about it happening so frequently that they just brush it off as "normal" for them. Let me tell you, constipation is far from normal and can lead to a rectal tear or prolapse if they are straining for a significant period of time.

The good news is that with potbelly pigs treating constipation usually is very simple and straight forward. The main reason for constipation is *diet*. I'm sure your are tired of hearing me stress the importance of their diet, but I have seen first hand in numerous pigs how a simple diet change can fix so many common issues people have with their pigs. *You need to make sure your pig is getting adequate fiber in their diet and not being fed bread, pasta or pastries.* Zucchini and green beans provide great fiber content and if you live in an area where coconut water literally grows on trees, that is a great option as well. If your pig was fed a new food that caused the constipation you can feed them canned pumpkin for relief. Just make sure it is *pure* pumpkin rather than pumpkin pie mix. I say that because I have made that error but thankfully I caught it before I fed it to them. The high fiber content plus the added moisture is very beneficial for constipation. Also ensure that your pig is drinking enough water. Lack of exercise is also a contributing factor so make sure your pig is getting their daily workout or Zumba routine on.

Occasionally there are cases where the constipation is something more serious such as a intestinal or rectal tumor. Pigs are also very curious animals so there is always the possibility of a foreign body obstruction. This can occur from your pig eating a toy or other object that isn't meant for eating. If you notice any toys missing and are concerned about the possibility of them eating it, a quick radiograph at your vet may be a good idea to confirm if it is inside them or not.

If a foreign body obstruction is left untreated it can lead to an intestinal perforation, which has a very low survival rate. If constipation does not improve or is accompanied by blood and/or vomiting, your pig needs to be seen immediately.

Vomiting

Vomiting in pigs is rare, but if vomiting does occur they need to be seen as soon as possible. There are many people that will tell you that pigs physically can't vomit - and I promise you they can! It is one of the most foul odors but more importantly it is a symptom that should be taken seriously. Pigs don't just vomit once and go on their merry way. Vomiting is generally followed by lethargy and inappetence, both which are a serious sign that they need treatment. If your pig is vomiting, let them finish without picking them up as this often leads to aspiration pneumonia.

Salt Toxicity

Salt toxicity in pigs is a very serious condition which causes neurologic disturbances and even death. The symptoms can start out with mild lethargy then proceed to CNS signs such as ataxia, blindness, seizures or confusion. Cerebral edema can also occur and needs to be treated immediately.

Salt toxicity can be caused by eating salty foods - potato chips are not meant for pigs no matter how cute it is to watch them eat them! With that being said, the most common reason for salt toxicity in mini pigs is actually water deprivation. This causes high sodium levels in their body. When a pig has not had water, either from their water bowl running out and having it go unnoticed, or from intentionally limiting their water intake, when water is finally offered they will drink like they have been parched for weeks. It's just their nature and nearly all of them will do it. A pig consuming a large amount of water at once can be just as deadly as elevated sodium levels within the body.

The reason I mentioned one of the factors being "intentionally limiting their water intake" is because unfortunately it happens very frequently with mini pigs living inside the home. Pigs like to go from food to water, food to water causing a

mess sometimes, or dribbling water across the floor if they take a drink then get excited and go running to something more entertaining across the room. Whatever the case may be: DO NOT EVER WITHHOLD WATER FROM YOUR PIG. In the event that their water bowl gets tipped over accidentally and it went unnoticed start filling it back up 1/2 cup at a time every 30 minutes, rather than all at once.

Lameness

Potbelly pigs are prone to lameness issues partially because of their conformation, but more commonly due to being overweight.

Overgrown or cracked hooves can also contribute to lameness issues in your pig. Hoof trimming is not a quick fix when your pig becomes lame, rather something that is very important to keep up with so your pig doesn't get to that point. If the lameness is due to a hoof issue, it can often take time to resolve since their hooves don't grow very fast. Wet hooves can cause issues just as easy as dry, cracked hooves can. When hooves stay saturated, most likely from standing in mud, it is a breeding ground for infection and abscesses within the hoof. Iodine can be applied to the bottom of the hoof as antiseptic after they have been standing in the mud. Hoof dressing can be applied to cracked hooves. Make sure to clean all dirt or mud from the hoof first.

Fractures, sprains and strains are becoming a more common cause of lameness in mini pigs as they are becoming more popular as house pets. When your pig learns about all of the plush sleeping options around the house watch out! Jumping off of a couch or loosing their footing on a tile floor while going to jump up on a chair can quickly lead to a fractured limb. Non-slip rugs can help, but ultimately it is up to you if you want to teach them to jump on the couch to begin with.

[Maybelline has had a few close calls trying to jump into the bathtub, which is something that she taught herself when she was upset that I was taking a bath and she wasn't. I've have had to become a little more strict but it's hard *sometimes to discipline her without laughing; "No Ma'am - get off of the bathtub!"]*

Arthritis is also a cause of lameness, particularly in mature pigs. I'm sure it doesn't come as a surprise to you but the number one contributing factor to arthritis in pigs is obesity. Infectious arthritis can also cause lameness, such as if your pig ever contracted Erysipelas, so make sure to inform your vet if that is a possibility.

There are anti-inflammatories and for some cases joint injections that can be prescribed for treatment, so have them examined to get them back to their normal self as soon as possible. The longer a lameness issue goes untreated, the longer it can put strain on other muscles and ligaments, causing even greater damage.

Cystitis (+/- Bladder Stones)

Potbelly pigs are diagnosed with cystitis and bladder stones more commonly than you would expect. Cystitis is inflammation of the bladder, typically due to infection. It can certainly occur without the presence of bladder stones, although they both have a similar onset of symptoms. If you notice that your pig is having frequent urination, bloody urine, or straining to urinate, that could indicate one of these conditions. Cystitis will usually resolve after a round of antibiotics but it is a good time to have a urinalysis done. Having a urinalysis done at this time will be able to tell you if it is simply a bout of cystitis or if there are crystals in the urine as well. The presence of microscopic crystals in the urine is an indication that stones have already formed in the bladder, or are in the process of forming. If caught early enough you can typically change the pH of the urine via a prescribed diet or medication from your vet to help dissolve the crystals. If it is too late and the bladder stones are well-formed, surgery may be the only option to remove them. This can be very painful for your pig so you may notice a change in their attitude along with the other symptoms of these conditions.

Heat Exhaustion

Heat exhaustion is a very serious condition that can come on very quickly in pigs due to their inability to sweat. Pigs need to have at minimum, a shaded area and water to be able to cool off in if they are outdoors. When the humidity levels are high the risk is even higher for your pig to get overheated.

If you notice your pigs activity level decreasing in the heat you need to take action to get them to a cooler area - preferably in air conditioning. If your pig is showing advanced symptoms of heat exhaustion, such as lethargy, open-mouth breathing or panting, they need to be taken to the vet immediately before further internal damage occurs. In the mean time you can initiate cooling measures by wetting them down with water and placing bags of frozen peas (or similar) under their armpits and in their inguinal area between their rear legs. Do not submerge them in ice as this can cause them to go into shock. As always, make sure fresh water is available at all times.

Toxin Exposure

Food Toxicity

Yes, even pigs are susceptible to food-related toxins. There are the common foods to avoid listed in the nutrition section, although I'm sure there are other foods that are not recommended to be fed to pigs depending on what region you are in, with different native fruits and such. Make sure to do your research on a new food prior to feeding it to your pig if there is any question at all if it is ok for them. Even though you *shouldn't feed* your pig bread, it isn't toxic to them ... bread dough on the other hand can actually have a toxic effect on them. If a pig is given bread dough, the yeast in a moist, warm environment (stomach) will expand and continue to ferment. Moldy food is also very toxic to pigs contrary to how hearty of a reputation they have of being able to eat anything. Do not ever give your pig any moldy or fermented food.

Cyanide

Cyanide poisoning obviously isn't going to surprise you as being a toxic substance. Pigs can get Cyanide poisoning from ingesting fertilizers or pesticides, so make sure to keep them up and out of reach of your curious pig. Use caution if you need to spray pesticides on your property, keep your pig inside while spraying and let it completely dry before letting your pig walk on it. Some of the chemicals will say "safe for animals after 30 minutes of drying" but that only means to walk on. Keep in mind that a pig may also try to eat the grass where you sprayed, which I promise you isn't safe at anytime.

The same goes for any other toxic substances typically kept in garages or barns that your pig could get into such as anti-freeze, gasoline, motor oil, etc. A bag simply rolled up is not enough to deter them, as they are very curious about things like that. All products need to be elevated and completely out of reach of your pig.

Rat Bait

If you have other animals, I'm sure you have heard it stressed time and time again to keep any rat bait or rodenticides well out of reach. The same holds true for your pig. Rat bait can quickly cause internal bleeding, cerebral edema and other serious medical issues, frequently leading to death if untreated. The internal damage can begin before you notice symptoms, although seizures, muscle tremors and ataxia can often be seen following ingestion. It has a flavor meant to attract rodents which means that most other animals are attracted to it as well. If your pig accidentally eats even a very small amount you will need to get them to the vet as soon as possible in order for them to either induce emesis, or other means of removing it. Make sure to bring the packaging with you because different rodenticide ingredients call for different detox treatments.

Human Drugs

Human drugs (legal or not) can pose great harm to your pig, especially a little pig. As bitter as some prescription drugs are, I have seen numerous cases of pigs consuming a whole bottle of human medications. I'm not sure what is so appealing to them - maybe it is the enjoyment of opening the bottle and then it looks like food to them so they eat it? Many of the medications are absorbed and start working quickly which is bad news for your pig, so keep them far out of reach. If they accidentally get ahold of medication, detoxifying treatment will most likely need to be initiated.

I shouldn't even need to mention this but since I have seen it happen, I suppose there is someone else out there who might try it. Getting your pig drunk, stoned or high is not cute or funny in any way shape or form. Nearly all street drugs will flat out kill your pig or cause long-term neurologic defects.

Plants

There are many plants, trees and grasses which are toxic to your pig. There are definitely more plants in the world than I can list here so *please* do your research prior to feeding your pig any plants or allowing the plants or shrubbery to grow near their pasture. A few commonly growing toxic plants include: Cannabis, Poinsettia, Locoweed, Mustard plant/seeds, Bamboo and Cocoa (any part, including the husks.)

~

Death & Dying

This isn't a subject I like to focus on much, but since many of the questions I receive are about the death or terminal illness of someone's pet pig I will touch on it.

There will come a time when you will have to say goodbye. Unfortunately this is a fact of life. No matter how much you prepare for it I can't say that it ever gets any easier. Preparing yourself mentally can help with the grieving process though. Even being in the veterinary field for quite some time now, seeing death and dying on a regular basis, I still take it very hard when I have to say goodbye to a pig, even if it is someone else's pig.

Sometimes you will not get a chance to prepare or say goodbye and that is a struggle as well. I like to think in cases like theses they didn't have anytime to suffer or endure a painful illness. Sometimes you will loose a pig who is way too young to even be remotely ready. If it helps with closure you can elect to have a necropsy done in hopes to determine the cause of death, but also know that it could be a heart defect that they were born with and there was no way to fix it if you tried.

It is important to take time to grieve and everyone handles it differently. The most important thing you need to understand after loosing your pet pig is that you gave them the best life possible. If you are reading this book and are so much as making a pig a pet to begin with - then they are a whole lot better off than the greater population of the pigs in this world. You loved them and cared for them and all the silly memories you have of them will remain in your heart forever. You did a great job and I know they loved you just as much. Rely on faith, family and friends (even if they are 4-legged) to get you through tough times.

The Little Book of Little Pigs

Chapter 7

Big Pigs

"Horse Kisses"

"Doo Doo Happens" It may camouflage well but one of my assistants got sprayed with pig diarrhea while we were working overseas, which we later found out was full of Pinworms. Needless to say, we successfully dewormed the piglet and his litter mates!

Found some "little" big pigs who needed veterinary care while working overseas in Rabaul.

Examining and providing much needed preventative care to a pig in Nicaragua.

I wanted to briefly touch on ownership of *big* pigs as well since one of my first pet pigs was a Hampshire pig named "Cowgirl." She was the runt of a large litter and when I got her she only weighed about 2 pounds. I have to say that even though she wasn't a potbellied pig, she was one of my favorites . She stayed in the house until she got too big, but seemed to enjoy it more in the barn anyway. She still was allowed to come inside when she wanted to and always had fresh meals. Cowgirl was equally as smart as the mini pigs I have had and loved to lay around under the big shade tree with the dogs.

Hampshires and other large breed pigs typically grow to 300-400 pounds, although some have topped the scales in the 500-700 pound range. Their size makes it difficult to be housed inside your home as a pet pig, although they can still make great companions.

Many of the housing and nutritional guidelines are the same in large and small breed pigs. Since they are typically kept outside in a barn due to their size, it is important to monitor them just as closely as a pig you would keep inside. Any changes in weight, attitude, or activity level should be promptly addressed.

Many of the problems found in large breed pigs who are housed outdoors are caused by poor husbandry practices. People tend to get the mentality that because the pig is outdoors they need to be a muddy sloppy mess all the time and act like a "pig." While pigs do enjoy laying in the mud or in a small pool of water on a hot day to stay cool, it needs to be kept clean. Mud is a breeding ground for parasites which can lead to many internal and external health problems.

I know I have already mentioned it, but pigs are *very* clean animals. Large or small pigs, old or young, they naturally try to be clean. Pigs are very particular about their restroom area and will usually only go in one area of their pen and even in one area of their litterbox. The reason that you see pig pens get so disgusting and dirty is because people do not clean their pens. If they are inside - wash their blankets and beds regularly just as you would a dog or other pet. It really is quite a simple fix.

Following the housing guidelines in this book will help eliminate the common problems caused by poor husbandry. Keep in mind that a larger pig will require a larger area to eat, sleep and play. Proper pasture management and rotation in large breed pigs is not an area to put on the back burner. It is such a vital aspect of keeping a pig healthy. A larger pig will root through a pasture much quicker than a mini pig, therefore depleting the nutrients quicker. This can be effectively managed by pasture rotation and not allowing too many pigs in the same pasture at once.

Working with your pig to accept frequent handling and teaching proper behavior when they are young is crucial in large breed pigs. Once they are full grown, restraint becomes very difficult and dangerous if they do not have respect for you.

[While working on a litter of pigs overseas there was a sow who had a history of having a very bad attitude so we separated her to the next pen over while we worked on her piglets. Before long she went flying over the concrete barrier wall, all 450 pounds of her, jaws wide open and bit one of the locals in the back. We pushed him out of the way just in time, otherwise he would have been missing much more of his back today. I didn't know pigs could fly but apparently they can.]

This particular case was a sow being very protective of her young. It is important to respect that and only handle the piglets for short periods of time to build the sow's trust that you aren't there to hurt them. It is also important to understand the potential damage and injury a pig can cause if they are not handled properly. Unfortunately I have also learned that a starved pig won't hesitate to take a chunk out of your boot or leg either to find food. Thankfully this isn't a frequent occurrence when pigs are fed regularly but always use caution.

If you get into a situation where you need to restrain a large pig make sure to go slow with them and most importantly do not chase them. You can slowly herd them into a small pen or chute for a more controlled environment to work with them.

There is also a device called a **hog snare** which is a long pole with an adjustable rope or wire on the end of it which is used for restraint. Position the rope through their mouth and over their snout before tightening. This device should be used for temporary control and restraint then released.

Chapter 8

My Little Piggy

Where To Start?

The reason "where to start" is at the end is because I want to make sure that all the possibilities of the good, the bad and the ugly have been understood. Without further adu - CONGRATS on your decision to embark on your piggy adventure! They really are intelligent creatures and are great fun to have as pets. There never seems to be a dull moment when they are around.

By far, the best place to start your search for a pig is through a rescue organization or humane society. Be diligent about this though and make sure that a "rescue" is legitimately that. A rescue should not be charging outrageous fees for adoption. There definitely are expenses involved, especially for pigs who have had their preventative care and have already been spayed/neutered but it shouldn't be astronomical. Currently the statistic is that 50% of potbelly pigs are rehomed within their first year which means there may be individuals in your area with a pig up for adoption, so take a look at your local ads as well.

If you are not having luck finding a pig via a rescue, you can look into finding a breeder. Make sure to do your homework in this department, as how your pig has been bred and raised for the first part of their life plays a vital role in their long-term health and wellbeing. Observe the cleanliness of the facility, overall impression of the other pigs and knowledge of the breeder. If it is a quality breeder, there should be no problem with you asking to see the sow and boar of your future pig. Keep in mind that pigs reach puberty much earlier than they stop growing, so a mother pig may only be 20 pounds but she also might only be 7 months old. Pigs will not reach their full-size until 2-3 years of age. They generally have a younger or older appearance to them, so after looking at multiple different pigs you should be able to get a general idea of their age by facial features, coat texture and tusk growth.

Pig Selection

If you have the option of selecting a pig from a litter, either from a shelter or a breeder, it can be a lot of fun. It's always interesting to stand back and observe them for a few minutes before they see you so you can get a feel for how they act in a group. They all have their different personalities and quirkiness. Observe anything abnormal about the other pigs, such as if a few of them have diarrhea, it is highly likely yours will too. As discussed earlier, this can be an early symptom of something more serious.

I tend to always go for the lone ranger or one with a medical or behavioral issue because I can usually work with it and enjoy fixing them. I will be honest with you though that going for the cute little lone ranger runt can be a major disappointment, as many have a significantly shortened life span. The ideal pig to select for your new pet will be socializing with the other pigs - although not overly dominant, appear to be in good health, playful and inquisitive.

It is beneficial to do a brief exam while you are at the farm, checking for any lice, alopecia, itching, or other abnormal findings on their skin, healthy weight, ability to walk in a straight line without tilting their head or circling, no nasal discharge, coughing, drooling or sneezing, normal stools, and overall happiness. Most of these things you can work with but it is always better to start with a healthy pig instead of taking the risk of bringing a potentially contagious disease into your home or property.

Bringing Home Your New Pig

Hopefully you will already have an area set up for your pig for when you bring them home. I do understand though that there are a few others out there like me who may leave for work in the morning and end up coming home with a new pet pig by the end of the day. In that case you can improvise - a bathtub with a non-slip bath mat and blanket will suffice temporarily.

Wherever your pig gets to stay when they first arrive home, make sure it is quiet so they don't get too stressed out. I know it can be a very exciting time, especially if this is your first pig or if you have children but try to give your pig a little bit of time to settle in before they are introduced to too many new people or animals. Introducing the litterbox can begin the day they get home but I wouldn't stress too many other new things on them such as harness and leash training the first week.

After the first week mark I would recommend taking them in for an initial vet visit to get caught up on any preventative care they haven't had, including a fecal analysis to check for any intestinal parasites. This is a good time to get acquainted with your pig vet if you haven't already. From day one it is always a good idea to keep thorough medical records on your pig of any veterinary care or treatment they receive. You can also keep a record of their normal vitals as well. Hopefully you will be provided with a previous medical history from wherever you get your pig from but that is always easier said than done. It's never to late to start a record though. This will help you precisely track your pig's health and observe any abnormal trends.

"Bourbon" and "Ginger" already making friends.

"Bourbon" 2 year old male mini-pig making himself at home in the spare bedroom shortly after arriving.

Conclusion

So I guess it is nothing less than par for the course to have a new piggy arrive the night I finish this book. "Bourbon" arrived just as I was going to submit this book for publishing so I figured I would make an addendum and introduce him as well.

"Bourbon" is a 2 year old miniature potbelly pig who has a heart of gold and loves attention. Only 30 minutes after arriving last night I already thought that I lost him! Needless to say, he had already found the spare bedroom and made himself at home on the bed, under the pillows. Well then, welcome to the family! He slept in the spare bedroom all night and only got a little grumpy when I turned on the bright lights once in the middle of the night, and again this morning to check on him.

He finally decided it was time to get up and start the day. Bourbon made his way to the litterbox without me showing him where it was then enjoyed some banana flaxseed oatmeal for breakfast. There was a little scuffle at breakfast when Maybelline tried to steal his oatmeal but he handled it like a champ and picked up his bowl to run off. What else do you do when someone tries to steal your oatmeal?

I hope that one way or another this book has given you some insight as to what to expect if you choose to open your home up to a pet pig. I hope that if you do choose to get a pig that you can enjoy it as much as I do. Clearly I have accidentally created somewhat of a rescue facility for any animal in need, especially pigs over the recent years. In all actuality though, it was a dream of mine since I was a little girl to take in and help any animal in need and to live out those dreams, even on a smaller scale feels great. I hope to continue to pursue this dream and exponentially expand my animal rescue facility and capabilities.

I suppose that goes without saying that a majority of the proceeds from this book will be allocated for enhancing the life of pigs in need.

Medical Chart

Name: _____ Sex: _____ DOB __/__/___

Color: _____ Breed: _____

Vitals

Date	Temperature	Pulse	Respirations	Weight
__/__/__	_____	_____bpm	_____bpm	_____
__/__/__	_____	_____bpm	_____bpm	_____
__/__/__	_____	_____bpm	_____bpm	_____
__/__/__	_____	_____bpm	_____bpm	_____
__/__/__	_____	_____bpm	_____bpm	_____
__/__/__	_____	_____bpm	_____bpm	_____
__/__/__	_____	_____bpm	_____bpm	_____
__/__/__	_____	_____bpm	_____bpm	_____
__/__/__	_____	_____bpm	_____bpm	_____
__/__/__	_____	_____bpm	_____bpm	_____
__/__/__	_____	_____bpm	_____bpm	_____

Vaccines

Date	Type & Location	Amount	Reaction
__/__/__	_____	_____ml	_____

Vial Label:

| __/__/__ | _____ | _____ml | _____ |

Vial Label:

| __/__/__ | _____ | _____ml | _____ |

Vial Label:

| __/__/__ | _____ | _____ml | _____ |

Vial Label:

| __/__/__ | _____ | _____ml | _____ |

Vial Label:

| __/__/__ | _____ | _____ml | _____ |

Vial Label:

| __/__/__ | _____ | _____ml | _____ |

Vial Label:

Vaccines

Date	Type & Location	Amount	Reaction
__/__/__	_____	_____ ml	_____

Vial Label:

| __/__/__ | _____ | _____ ml | _____ |

Vial Label:

| __/__/__ | _____ | _____ ml | _____ |

Vial Label:

| __/__/__ | _____ | _____ ml | _____ |

Vial Label:

| __/__/__ | _____ | _____ ml | _____ |

Vial Label:

| __/__/__ | _____ | _____ ml | _____ |

Vial Label:

| __/__/__ | _____ | _____ ml | _____ |

Vial Label:

Deworming

Date	Type	Amount	Fecal Results
__/__/__			
__/__/__			
__/__/__			
__/__/__			
__/__/__			
__/__/__			
__/__/__			
__/__/__			
__/__/__			
__/__/__			
__/__/__			
__/__/__			
__/__/__			
__/__/__			
__/__/__			
__/__/__			
__/__/__			
__/__/__			
__/__/__			

Hoof Care

Date	Description	Notes
01/01/15	ex. Full trim completed by farrier Fred	Hooves dry - applied hoof oil
__/__/__		
__/__/__		
__/__/__		
__/__/__		
__/__/__		
__/__/__		
__/__/__		
__/__/__		
__/__/__		
__/__/__		
__/__/__		
__/__/__		
__/__/__		
__/__/__		
__/__/__		
__/__/__		

Dental Care

Date	Anesthetic Used	Procedure
__/__/__	_____	_____
__/__/__	_____	_____
__/__/__	_____	_____
__/__/__	_____	_____
__/__/__	_____	_____
__/__/__	_____	_____
__/__/__	_____	_____
__/__/__	_____	_____
__/__/__	_____	_____
__/__/__	_____	_____
__/__/__	_____	_____
__/__/__	_____	_____
__/__/__	_____	_____
__/__/__	_____	_____

Illness

Date	Diagnosis	Treatment Received

__/__/__   _____   _____

Notes: _____

Hospitalized Y / N   **Date Resolved:** __/__/__

~

__/__/__   _____   _____

Notes: _____

Hospitalized Y / N   **Date Resolved:** __/__/__

~

__/__/__   _____   _____

Notes: _____

Hospitalized Y / N   **Date Resolved:** __/__/__

~

__/__/__   _____   _____

Notes: _____

Hospitalized Y / N   **Date Resolved:** __/__/__

~

__/__/__   _____   _____

Notes: _____

Hospitalized Y / N   **Date Resolved:** __/__/__

Notes

_____

_____

_____

_____

_____

_____

_____

_____

_____

_____

_____

_____

_____

_____

Notes

_____

_____

_____

_____

_____

_____

_____

_____

_____

_____

_____

_____

_____

_____

_____

Little Pig Diary

_____, ____ *(date)*

_____
_____
_____
_____
_____
_____

_____, ____ *(date)*

_____
_____
_____
_____
_____
_____

_____, ____ *(date)*

_____
_____
_____
_____
_____
_____

The Little Book of Little Pigs

_____, ____ *(date)*

_____
_____
_____
_____
_____
_____

_____, ____ *(date)*

_____
_____
_____
_____
_____
_____

_____, ____ *(date)*

_____
_____
_____
_____
_____
_____

The Little Book of Little Pigs

_____, ____ *(date)*

_____
_____
_____
_____
_____
_____

_____, ____ *(date)*

_____
_____
_____
_____
_____
_____

_____, ____ *(date)*

_____
_____
_____
_____
_____
_____

The Little Book of Little Pigs

_____, ____ (date)

_____
_____
_____
_____
_____
_____

_____, ____ (date)

_____
_____
_____
_____
_____
_____

_____, ____ (date)

_____
_____
_____
_____
_____
_____

88666936R00086

Made in the USA
Columbia, SC
02 February 2018